Clear Investing, Intentional Investing

Robert Schmansky, MA, CFP®

To all of those whose lives I have been able to witness, advise, assist, learn from, collaborate with, who helped put together the pieces of what personal investment services could be.

Table of Contents

Clear Investing, Intentional Investing

Clear Investing, Intentional Investing

As a financial advisor, I've seen it all. In serving, speaking with, and advising hundreds of investors, while working at financial institutions, planning firms, and with my own firm, Clear Financial Advisors, I've seen investors make the same mistakes time and time again. In portfolio construction mistakes that are often costlier than people understand.

The following stories are based on interactions with clients:

> ⟩ Mike and Susan paid to have a financial plan prepared. At the end of the analysis many recommendations for various products were made. The plan they paid for seemed to meet their goals, but in the products that were recommended would cost over 3% than was projected for in the reports... *if this situation sounds familiar see the chart on page 8 on the damage that costs can have on a plan.*

> ⟩ Jack is concerned about the amount of money his mother has in an FDIC-insured certificate of deposit. Discussing this with his financial advisor, the recommendation was to move the account to a so-called 'safe' investment that could earn more quite a bit more. The strategy had never lost money before, Jack remembered hearing from the advisor. When the account was down 4%, the advisor told Jack, "Don't worry. They will be working extra hard to make that up by the end of the year"... *if this sounds like something you may have heard, keep reading to learn about Gambling, Investment Principles, and Absolute Return strategies.*

> ⟩ Stephen, recently widowed, was never interested in the family investment plan. While seeking to increase his investment yield, he met with an advisor who recommend he change his mutual fund manager. When this manager failed to produce results and the

rating service reduced its grading on them, he was introduced to a new fund manager. Each time there was a manager change it was because the client lost much more than a basic, market portfolio. His advisor continued the process of recommending '4 star' or '5 star' mutual funds which did worse than average once he invested... *Gambling, mutual fund manager performance games, and the unintentional risks that exist with star ratings are covered later.*

➤ Mary is a diligent saver, and puts as much as she can into her employer's 401(k). While receiving a match on her funds is a bonus, she does not realize her plan costs over 2%, and so does not research other available investment options. Upon retirement she leaves the money in her employer plan since it has 'no costs.' At retirement, she discusses her options with the 401(k) company (also an insurer) who puts her money into one of the company's proprietary annuities... *while on the outside this seems like a safe approach, keep reading to learn about the lack of diversification risks related to having a 100% Stability portfolio, and if your retirement plan is the best place to save.*

These individuals made mistakes that are not necessarily obvious, nor will the consequences necessarily appear to be significant at the time, but the end result was often a substantial impact on their portfolio and risk level. I've seen individuals who, by listening to what seemed to be good advice, cut their portfolios and future income streams by *half* or greater.

Consider the magnitude of that for a moment. While we all want to have a successful experience with our hard earned investment dollars, yet we are prone to making the same mistakes others have made, and professionals have tried to warn us about many times over. There isn't anything particularly unique about individuals who take on too much risk, in fact most do in one way or another, which is why I say most invest *unintentionally*. They believe they are doing a good thing, but are unaware of the potential risks of the strategy they've been sold.

These mistakes take many forms – mistaken philosophies and beliefs about how money works, and actions we take to try to correct previous mistakes. Since there isn't a lot with investing that hasn't been tried before, as an advisor it can be particularly upsetting to see the same setbacks to clients' financial plans.

Why do we continue to make mistakes many have made before? With all who have been down this road ahead of us, shouldn't we have a better understanding of what it means to invest successfully?

The truth is, there are a number of reasons why we continue to allow bad ideas to impact our portfolio plans. We aren't taught about money or investments and so we tend to practice on ourselves. While we may spot a good article, or book, it doesn't tend to tie all of the pieces together in a coherent way for a personalized plan.

In meetings with clients, I have always wanted to have a tool to explain these mistaken beliefs to supplement the information and recommendations. I imagined it as something that clients could take home with them and refer to whenever an investment question presented, or represented, itself. *"I remember Rob explained exactly why we are doing this, but I just can't recall why."*

What I wanted was all of the data and charts at my fingertips that support the reasons behind positive actions we can make with our investments, as well as data that shows investment myths for what they are.

As I review the tools available, one thing was clear: there is *Too Much Information (TMI)* on investing available for consumption today. Just as I believe there is too much information besieging investors on a daily basis, there is a TMI problem for professional advisors as well. There are plenty of information providers that do a great job, but there is nothing comprehensive or specific to the job of explain the path investors should take and keeping them on that path. Retail sources of information – money magazines, television programs, and blogs – don't differ greatly from professional sources. They both are as often too general in nature to provide any real help.

In order to be useful, the information to help guide my clients had to fit very rigid requirements. It had to be accurate, true to investing principles, and explain these investment ideas and concepts to both the expert **and** the novice investor. Since I couldn't find both of these requirements elsewhere, I set out to write this book myself.

Investing information – good investing information – is hard to come by, and the reasons for the problem runs several layers deep:

➤ First, the financial media has the unenviable job of constantly capturing the public interest. You only sell your magazine if you make more incredible claims than the others on the rack. *The Top 7 Funds You Need to Own Today!... Double Your Investing Income!... Invest Like Warren Buffett!*

Too often these types of stories disseminate information which isn't based on investing principles, but rather promotes investing fads and fallacies. There are great financial writers, television commentators and publications, but too much of what is published today is meant to entertain rather than educate and inform.

➤ Another part of the problem – and speaking still about financial entertainment – is when we consider who we can trust for financial advice, we tend to think of 'financial celebrities' on talk and TV shows.

No financial celebrity gives advice that is blatantly harmful. But, they make a lifestyle out of simple slogans and generic advice, whereas your situation just may be complex and require someone understand your specific circumstances. Is it possible that advice that fits the needs of many, isn't right for you?

➤ Realizing now that television is effective at reaching investors, there is far too much information from commentators and professionals that simply put do not work with a mind toward **personal** finances. The newsmakers are the flashy investment managers who love to pontificate on the direction of the markets, but 100% of the time they fail to point out that their skills are better suited for institutional investors, rather than individuals and families. Investing as an individual requires a completely different paradigm than investing for a pension plan or institution, yet, most managers fail to acknowledge this basic truth in their commentary.

➤ And finally, in this media driven financial advice world, those that truly can make a difference are the ones who are not trusted. In a 2011 survey conducted by Forresters, two out of three clients of Merrill Lynch disagreed with the statement – *"My financial provider does what's best for me, not just its own bottom line."*

Not all financial advisors work for Merrill Lynch or in a similar brokerage-based business model, but it is true that financial advisors often have made considerations for the goals of third parties in advising individuals, rather than simply advising on what is in **your** best interest. Certain advisor associations are working to change that, but it does not help when a few bad apples set the expectations of the public.

What it all boils down to is that most individuals, whether working with an advisor or not, do not have the information they need to create an intentional plan for their money. They may hear parts from the news, but they just as likely have picked up irrelevant information. They might have seen an advisor for a fancy retirement calculation, but when it comes to the important task of implementing, they take, or are taken on, another path than the one their plan lays out for them.

Implementation Error

"Neo, sooner or later you're going to realize just as I did that there's a difference between knowing the path and walking the path." – The Matrix, 1999

When I refer to unintentional investing, what I mean is a failure to implement an investment plan from the planning stage to the investing stage by following the path your goals and planning dictated.

Too often a prospective client will come to the office with a great financial plan, one where the calculations and assumptions discuss and show theory that makes sense… but the execution looks *nothing* like what the plan detailed! It is almost as if these clients went to two different financial advisors – one who created the plan, developed the route to take, and another who decided to throw the plan out the window and improvise.

Consider if you were in charge of your households grocery list. You are diligent about planning for the week ahead, watching what you have and what is running out. When you go to the store to implement your list, to buy the groceries you need for the home, you shred the list and buy what you felt like at that moment. Maybe you stock up on microwave pizza, and forget about the fruit, vegetables, and everything else you might need for the rest of the week.

If you think you would have an angry spouse or partner at home after a grocery snafu, wait until they find out about the outcome of purchasing high-cost, ineffective investment strategies!

And even though this approach appears to make no sense at all – after all, you would think the advisor who created your plan would want to follow it with your investments – if you understand where we receive advice, and the background of the financial services industry, it's not surprising that product sales are still the driver of financial plans. The history of many financial advisory firms today are strongly connected to the financial product world. Firms or advisors may have started in the insurance, brokerage, or banking industries where the goal of advice was to sell a specific financial product. Even if advisors have become 'independent,' many never stop promoting these products due to relationships they have formed and retained.

Today I see a mishmash of financial advice based in one part on solid theories, and, in another part, the goals of these product firms and advisors. Some parts of accepted theory have been adapted into the analysis of most firms in the industry, but often only the parts that can be used to arrive at the same ending point – more sales. <u>The diagnosis may be correct</u>, **but** *the prescription is always to take two of these and call me when you have the money to buy two more.* The same investment prescription simply cannot be the solution to each individual financial situation.

Poor investment implementation makes both the implementation, and the advice, wrong. Nonsense. Worthless.

Think about a time you were planning a very important trip. You had a plan and route laid out. But, when it was time to set off, what if you make a last minute decision to leave the map at home and improvise? Maybe you'll end up at your destination, maybe you'll end up somewhere else.

Would it make any sense at all to plan if you had no intention of following the map? Of course not. And yet planning and not following through on an implementation plan that meets the needs of your plan is what most investors do. Not intentionally of course, they often believe the advisor who sold them the map is also guiding them down the right road.

With so much at stake for individuals, I wrote *Clear Investing, Intentional Investing* to provide an overview of personal investing strategy, in an easy to digest book. There is too much information from advisors, Wall Street, and even the financial press, whose flashy, but often irrelevant stories dismiss information that is necessary for individuals to understand their finances. It is my goal to collect and provide information that will help keep you on the path you mean to be on.

Financial Advice Cost

The costs of financial advice are simply staggering. I'm not even referring to those of you who hire financial advisors, I mean for YOU who:

> ➤ Invest in a company retirement plan, where you are held captive to the investing knowledge and choices of your employer,

> ➤ Hold a mutual fund where the company pays excessive costs to transact securities,

> ➤ Open an investment account with the bank or brokerage company.

Costs are not measured by direct fees alone. The potential growth on your investments that you miss out on, the opportunity cost from having to use a poor retirement plan for example, is a cost to you as well.

Most often, the information we need to make decisions about the cost of our investments is hidden, or at least very difficult to find, and so there is little measureable way for investors to make sound cost / value decisions. It isn't possible in this booklet to cover all costs associated with retirement plans, and so my goal is to plant seeds on what a reasonable cost solution may look like, so that you can consider it against your own plan. My hope is that this will encourage some to take a deeper look at their current investment strategy, and promote a more in depth conversation with their advisor about how the costs of your plan will impact the returns. I hope to also provide you with enough information to have a conversation about your financial plan with your advisor to determine if the advice you receive is leading you down a path toward a solid, intentional investment plan, or just window dressing to manage your money the way they were going to anyhow.

The following graph demonstrates the effect of fees on otherwise similar investment approaches. All three are meant to achieve the same returns, but we can see that the costs over time can have a material impact on your financial success.

Fees Matter

Assumed 6.5% Annualized Return over 30 Years

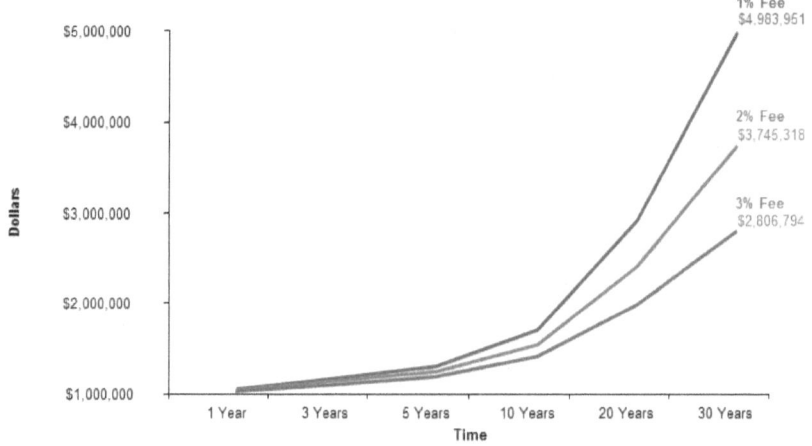

A 1% fee here not only refers to your advisors fee, but all of the costs of the investments they recommend, both the explicit (mutual fund management costs, broker transaction fees) and implicit (internal transaction fees the mutual fund). 1% in fees can be considered very low.

Many investors' costs can easily add up to around 2% (which can be relatively inexpensive). Most mutual funds exceed this limit on their own. The incremental increase from a 1% fee to 2% would reduce your portfolio by $1,200,000 over 30 years.

Can you think of anything to do with an extra $1,200,000? I know I certainly can!

Now, consider a fee that is very realistic for many investors of 3%. Many retirement plans by themselves have costs approaching this. At 3%, you have now lost $2,100,000 after 30 years. In 30 years $2,100,000 may not buy all that it does today, but it still should be an amount worth caring about.

With the average cost of an advisor being 1.32% before the costs of products, it is clear you should expect value for the amount you pay. But, how do you measure value? Knowing your investment plan may be costing you $2,100,000, you may be reconsidering how much they do!

My goal here is not to say advice isn't worth the cost… *very often it is!* You may not have implemented the correct plan to achieve the results above, or, you may find that you need the assistance to put together the right plan, and in those cases the costs are worthwhile.

But, you need to understand that what you are paying for is actually a part of the plan, and not simply an outcome the advisor would have come to no matter what. Their intention was to buy that pizza and so they forget the grocery list; they wanted to take you on a tour of the east coast and so while you wanted a map to a different destination, they didn't plan for your needs.

Through an understanding of *what* your advisor is doing for you, or the *motivations* of the information you are receiving elsewhere, *Clear Investing, Intentional Investing* will give you the tools to have a conversation about the actual costs of your plan, both in terms of total fees paid today and over your lifetime.

A Guide for What Works

This book is first and foremost meant to be a guide to what works, whether you do things yourself, or work with an advisor. It seeks to answer questions and provide *ah-hah* moments that make you realize the motivations of, and question the information you consume from the print or TV news, and even your financial advisor.

That being said, let me not hide the fact that this book is pro-advisor. Advisors (good ones) provide value in specific ways:

➤ *As a co-pilot* in the cockpit with you. No matter who is at the controls, there are two people whose opinions and observations help steer the course.

➤ *As a doctor,* there to provide expert information, diagnose problems, and prescribe solutions. However, just like a doctor is there when needed, they do not need to be a regular focus of your life.

➤ *As a coach* to provide the motivation, drills, and accountability to advance your plan.

➤ *As an architect;* an independent professional voice that builds your personalized plan.

I will share just a few of my personal experiences from working in financial planning practices, so that you can understand the value proposition of your advisor.

Likewise, I hope that this material will be understandable enough so that you can use it to proactively seek good advice. Advice is valuable. It helps us drop financial worries that so many learn to live with. **Imagine not having to create a myriad of sketches, notes, and spreadsheets to figure out your money; that your investment, tax, and insurance strategies are all in step with your overall financial plan; and that you had the time to live life to the fullest without financial worries.** That is what a good advisor should provide.

Two Purposes

Clear Investing, Intentional Investing is divided into two sections, each with its own purpose.

The first section, **Clear Investing**, provides information on the basics of investing in a way that is understandable and easy to consume. While this isn't a technical guide as much as a broad overview, my goal still is to provide information to the novice as well as the expert. For further information, I provide coverage on these topics frequently through media accessible through the email newsletter and my company's website at http://www.clearfa-llc.com/.

The second section, **Intentional Investing**, is meant to provide information for how to implement a successful investment plan. By successful I mean that these are the strategies that I have seen work, and, by contrast, strategies that ignore these ideas tend to place investment plans at risk of failure. Intentional Investing explains why ideas work or fail.

Background

My background is about as diverse as you can get in the financial services industry, and it is from that background that I've developed the *Clear Investing, Intentional Investing* philosophy. My career choices have led me to work for:

- A nationally known 'financial planning' company

- A regional bank

- A CPA firm

- An 'independent' fee-based advisor, who used a brokerage that was owned by an insurer. *Note: Fee-based advising is different from fee-only planning. Fee-based involves charging fees on products approved by brokers, and due to that relationship is not truly independent.*

- One of the largest independent money managers in the Midwest

- A 'holistic' planning firm

Why so many jobs? I like to believe that since I started out my intended career by studying financial planning, that I knew right out of school that what I wanted was a role that put people ahead of products and processes. Products are clearly a part of implementation, but selling them should not be the goal of a relationship. Rigid processes, slogans, rules of thumb, etc., just as much as products, also get in the way of providing a personal service. Some otherwise independent advisors cling to slogans and strategies that may work in one economic period or for one client, but not for another.

My first job was as an advisor with a national financial planning firm. I remember being thrilled to work with families toward better financial futures.

After meeting with my first prospective clients and putting together their financial plan, I had a review discussion of the strategy with my manager. His response was not quite as enthusiastic as I felt about finally presenting a plan to help clients achieve their goals.

What was wrong, he noted, was I needed to make sure I included certain investment product providers in the plan. It wasn't necessarily that he disagreed with the plan; it was that the execution of the plan with the investments needed to include more proprietary products and products that the firm was paid higher commissions on. He reworked the investment recommendations with those new funds.

Having felt I was compromising the trust my client had placed in me to make great recommendations, I wrote the branch manager a letter explaining my concerns with being more concerned about *product sales* than *advice*. His response was to kindly sit me down and state:

"Rob, if you want to sell XYZ Company products, I can approve you for a few of those products too."

This response wasn't exactly what I was looking for, <u>since my plan wasn't to sell XYZ Company products either</u>! In fact it was as if we were speaking an entirely different language. I was concerned about my ability to be unbiased, since I was being paid a fee specifically for advice, and I wanted to provide feedback that was useful and valuable, not just a roadmap to a product sale.

I learned a lot about the industry at that position and others. While that specific company had its roots as an insurer, and had now positioned itself and its ex-agents as financial advisors, not much changed as far as the company goals. Sell more of the insurers' mutual funds, annuities, and insurance products. However, now do it as an advisor instead of an insurance agent.

Due to my extensive experience working with different of financial advisors, I have a fairly unique understanding of the strengths, weaknesses, goals, and conflicts of the different models of advisory firm business models. It is from this understanding that I've formed the ideas in *Clear Investing, Intentional Investing* as those work for individual portfolio in the execution of the plan – the critical piece of the financial planning process that so many professionals and consumers historically fail at.

Needless to say, I believe that experience is invaluable for working with clients. I've seen great methods, poor methods, ineffective methods, and more than a few methods of providing advice services that didn't add much of anything to the plan or have an impact on client success. Because there are so many ways to approach a financial and investment plan, I've found that individuals need to learn how to question the ideas they come into contact with when implementing their plans. Sometimes simply following the advice of the person who created a 'financial plan' can lead to costly execution at best, and harmful at worst.

Clear Investing, Intentional Investing is a summary of the best practices I've learned along the way. In the following pages are truths about what a solid investment plan is, as well as myths that often trip us up and stall our progress. Myths have a tendency to be trendy; they come into vogue just after periods that they may have worked for a short time. But, myths always fail to meet investing principles and learning how to spot them will make the difference between having an intentional or an unintentional plan.

Principles

"[Principles] are natural laws that cannot be broken… The reality of such principles or natural laws becomes obvious to anyone who thinks deeply and examines the cycles of social history. These principles surface time and time again, and the degree to which people in society recognize and live in harmony with them moves them toward either survival and stability or disintegration and destruction." – The 7 Habits of Highly Effective People, Stephen R. Covey

Since we know advice that may not only take your best interests to heart does in fact exist, investors need to be diligent at determining if the advice they receive actually is appropriate for them.

It is of critical importance to have a basic foundation of knowledge from which to formulate questions before implementing an investment plan, or hiring an advisor to do so. You simply must understand the **principles** of investing before putting any plan into place; the costs are just too high to ignore.

If you don't start from a principled point, you become susceptible to harmful sales strategies that may sound like good ideas at the time.

Even if you do nothing with your investments, or manage them based on information you receive from the media, you are still exposed. There is just no way to avoid potentially harmful investing information.

Principles help us understand the world because they remove all of the white noise and allow us to judge an idea based on its adherence to known merits. The following are the four principles we will build upon throughout book, and return to, as we develop a plan to implement a real world, personal investment plan:

> ➤ **Principle #1: The financial markets work.** Technology has made it easy for anyone to be a participant in the markets. You can tap into the global financial markets today, from the comfort of your home, or from anywhere in the world on your smart phone.
>
> Those millions of participants determine prices of our stocks, bonds, and other security prices. Just like consumers decide on the prices of goods at the store based on supply and demand, the

same consumer forces regulates the prices of stocks and other securities.

Do stock prices react to news minute by minute, from changes in the expected growth of an economy, to the rising cost of commodity inputs? *You bet!*

The fact that prices change does not mean that they are wrong; they are in fact exactly right for that moment. Believing we have information that says that millions of buyers and sellers are wrong, but you are right is a flawed mindset to approach investing with.

➤ **Principle #2: Diversification is critical.** People have been and will continue to be wiped out by placing too much of their savings in one basket. Individually, investment assets are volatile. On the whole, they react much more smoothly. A diversified bucket of securities can protect your portfolio against the unknowns of any one specific security. Diversification, when done properly, can reduce volatility, while often maintaining or increasing returns.

➤ **Principle #3: If you want more return, you need to take more risk.** Higher return or yield is based on placing your investments at a higher risk. This realization supports the need to diversify in order to manage the risks of investments that have a higher chance of loss.

➤ **Principle #4: How you structure your portfolio explains your performance.** The way the investments are structured to provide growth and stability is responsible for most of the variability of portfolio returns. Structure trumps stock-picking and gambling as the way to create an investment plan based on known risk and return characteristics.

It is from these starting points that you can better understand your investments and drive conversations about your particular strategy with your advisor to ensure that your advice is in line with your goals and objectives.

Knowing your investment plan is a principled one is the piece investors need to bring to the table to achieve maximum comfort and control over your money.

Life becomes better when you are less concerned about money, and more in control of using it as a tool to achieve your goals. And, that is the reason you sought financial advice in the first place.

Clear Investing

What is Investing?

You may have heard investing defined as how much of your money to place into cash, bonds, and stock.

But that doesn't quite cover it. Investing is a lot more than a simple decision on how much to put into these areas of the market.

➤ First, it involves *understanding and making sound choices* regarding the vast number of products and strategies that make up what encompasses the activity of investing. We need to know if products are valid investments based on principle, or simply gimmicks and unsound strategies.

➤ Second, the decision on *how much cash to hold really isn't an investing decision at all*, and you should be wary if it seems like an advisor is making it one. Investing is often confused with saving, but the two are completely different and distinct activities. Though you need to consider your savings needs when deciding how much to invest, cash should not be a part of the investment plan, and you should not allow an advisor to charge you to 'invest' your cash under their management.

Beware of 'high-yield' cash, and 'cash alternatives.' Wall Street always wants to maximize the amount of your money they manage, but while they *may* know a thing or two about investing, they do not understand the concept of saving. Savings to Wall Street is the same as it was to the economist John Maynard Keynes – *an unnecessary drain on the economy and sales!*

Because the financial planning process often exposes all of your assets they frequently target cash. If you actually have too much cash then you should invest the excess; by that I mean you have more than a comfortable amount of emergency cash (6-12 months of expenses for most), in addition to any variable expenses (car replacement, kitchen upgrade fund) for the next three years in cash-like instruments.

Needless to say, if your advisor talks to you about enhancing your cash returns, or earning just a little more by investing your cash… **run, don't walk, for the door!** See the section later *Chasing Yield* to learn about investors who have lost a lot more than they anticipated by high-risk cash alternative investments.

➤ Third, *investing is more than placing money into investments at random.* Behind the decision what to buy should be a purpose. You should match your assets to your goals. An investment plan should be structured around goals first.

➤ Fourth, investing needs to be an activity that is based on evidence. We have expectations of return and risk. Many confuse the attempt to grow wealth through *investing* with *speculating* and *gambling*, likely in part due to the financial information problem, or due to working with advisors who are speculators or gamblers.

Speculating is different from investing, in it involves specialized knowledge that the speculator has (or believes he has) to attempt to make outsized gains, at the risk of outsized losses. **Gambling** is an activity that is an attempt to gain with little consideration of, but a huge opportunity for loss. Though there is little chance for total loss with most investment products, I refer to many money managers, financial advisors, and mutual funds later on as Gamblers mainly due to the lack of consideration for the appropriateness of an investment.

Investing for the Long(er) Term

Investing has the connotation as an activity for the long-term. By that I mean it is one that we will put into place and expect it to bear fruit over time by maintaining a disciplined approach to the strategy over market ups and downs. This does not imply that it is passively implemented, but rather that the strategy is based on principles, and is reviewed regularly to be sure it sticks to those guidelines.

The purpose of investing is to increase the value of your assets at a rate that surpasses inflation. How we get there is through a combination of investments that seek growth, purchasing power preservation, and dollar stable assets constructed in a manner to be a roadmap for intentional portfolio results.

G / P / S Investing™

Investing with Intention

Creating a plan for wealth involves deciding what assets should be included, having a methodology for ruling out investments that do not fit on principle or purpose, and building the portfolio in a way that makes sense for all of the nuances and advantages of your personal financial circumstances.

To start, let's cover the methodology I have created for determining the areas and investments we want to invest in – *G/P/S Investing*™.

G/P/S Investing™ gives us the guidelines for properly structuring a portfolio, and how to determine which investments are a fit. It allows us to choose investments based on their merits for meeting a goal of investors – growth, purchasing power preservation, and stability of their capital.

Growth / Preservation / Stability

What exactly should an investment plan for an individual look like?

Growth is what most people think of when we think investing. It is the opportunity for longer term growth of your money over inflation and safer investments.

But a portfolio of only growth investments simply isn't practical or appropriate for people. With the opportunity for high gains comes the certainty that there will be losses. Since individuals – unlike pension funds and money managers – do not have an infinite horizon for needing to use their money, it isn't appropriate to have a 100% growth portfolio for individuals without accounting for the possibility, no matter how small, that this money MAY need to be used.

Consider the chart below of the return of the market as compared to a risk-free asset from January 1990 to 2010. The average monthly excess return of the market is 0.52%; however the highest outperformance was 11.1%, and the lowest monthly difference between safety and the stock market was -18.6%.

Market Premium

Monthly: January 1990–December 2010

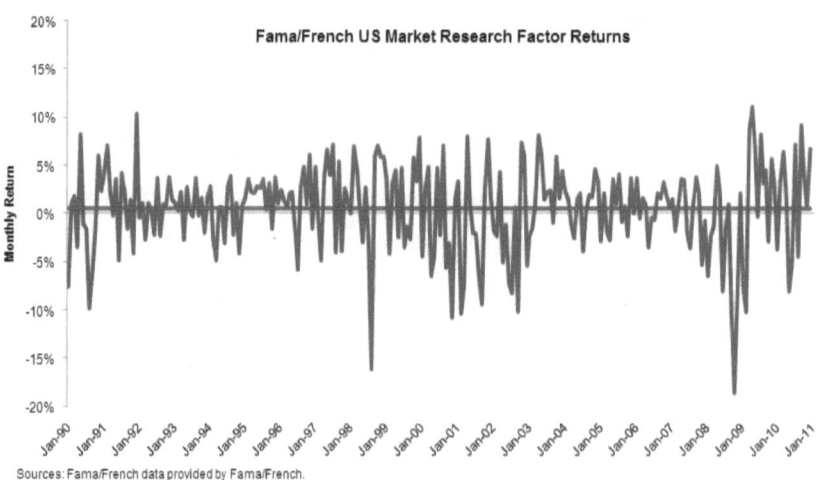

Fama/French US Market Research Factor Returns

Sources: Fama/French data provided by Fama/French.
Indices are not available for direct investment; their performance does not reflect the expenses associated with the management of an actual portfolio.
Past performance is not a guarantee of future results.

Stability is the next place investors turn. Stable investments don't deliver the results most investors need, but in combination with growth can provide for a less volatile investing experience.

Can we invest with just a portfolio of Growth AND Stability?

This has been the classic approach that can work for investors. A combination of growth and stability has been the benchmark that is taught in finance courses and most financial advisors have used it successfully for their clients.

I believe that there is a third motivation of investors that should be considered when constructing a portfolio – the consideration for the purchasing power **preservation** of a dollar. Stable assets simply do not keep up with the rising costs of living, and while Growth assets have over time, in the short-run they often do not.

Our goal in investing is to define the allocations to each of these purposes and select a mix of assets that have the attributes to meet those goals. In this way, *G/ P / S Investing*™ is your roadmap for portfolio construction and navigation.

The components of *G / P / S Investing*™ are Growth, Preservation, and Stability. Investors want their money to grow, they want the purchasing power of their money to rise, and they also want some portion of their money to be safe from risk.

G / P / S Investing™ allows an investor to create a portfolio that is intentional in its construction. It gives a framework for choosing investments based on whether or not they best meet our needs in one of the three categories. Over each category we still will want to diversify, but only with high quality investments that meet the criteria of the category. If an investment does not meet the principles of a category, we know it does not belong in your plan.

G / P / S Investing™ provides a clear way to see if an investment meets the requirements for inclusion in your portfolio, or if it is just another Wall Street gimmick product. Just like a G.P.S. system guides your way, *G / P / S Investing*™ will make sure your investment plan follows a sound route to your destination.

Let's start our review of a *G / P / S Investing*™ strategy by covering the Growth aspect of a portfolio.

Growth

Growth is meant to provide the greatest chance of increasing at a rate over the inflation rate over time. Growth is the excitement in the portfolio as it can quickly increase the bottom line, but it can also be a scary ride when the market turns in the other direction.

Growth is ownership of business through stocks or stock mutual funds.

Note: For purposes of this book I refer to Growth (capital G) as the ownership of equity, and not a subsection type of stocks. Our definition of Growth refers to the idea stocks are expected to grow faster than the rate of inflation over time. For advanced readers, I will discuss the benefits of having a tilt towards 'value' or high book-to-market companies within Growth.

Sensible growth is using growth in the context of a *G / P / S Investing*™ plan, and not simply investing in an aggressive growth only strategy.

Reasons to own:

Growth will go up, and it will go down, but, if we remember that within growth we own corporations whose management has the goal of maximizing profits (which you share in as an owner), it is clear that we should expect the value of our stocks to grow over periods of time.

Growth has provided the greatest return above inflation since companies have the ability to offer products at a price over the inflation rate. In the short-term, the price of a commodity used in the production of a product may fluctuate and have an effect on company profits. In the long-run, companies can make the changes required by the current economic conditions to achieve maximum profits. In the short-term, a company may not be able to change on a dime to deal with current economic realities, but in the long-run successful companies will change, grow, and react to new circumstances to meet growth targets.

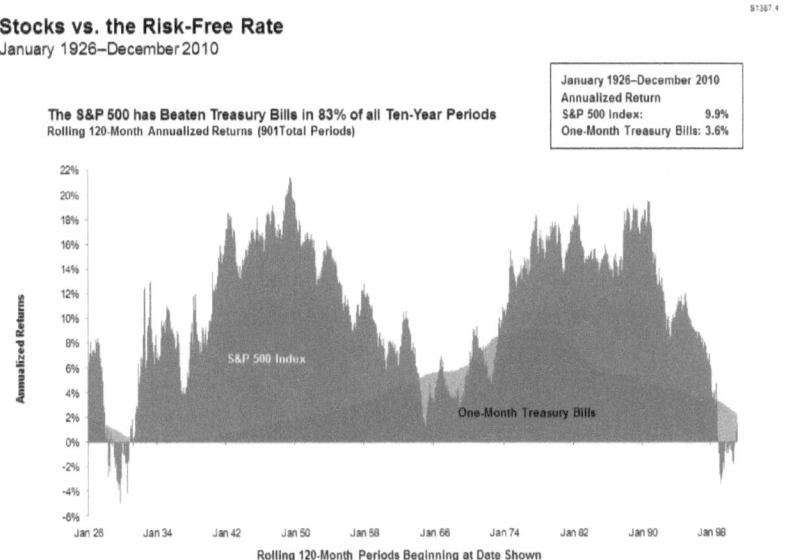

Stocks vs. the Risk-Free Rate
January 1926–December 2010

The S&P 500 has Beaten Treasury Bills in 83% of all Ten-Year Periods
Rolling 120-Month Annualized Returns (901 Total Periods)

The S&P data are provided by Standard & Poor's Index Services Group. US long-term bonds, bills, inflation, and fixed income factor data © Stocks, Bonds, Bills, and Inflation Yearbook™, Ibbotson Associates, Chicago (annually updated work by Roger G. Ibbotson and Rex A. Sinquefield).
Indexes are not available for direct investment. Their performance does not reflect the expenses associated with the management of an actual portfolio. Past performance is not a guarantee of future results. Not to be construed as investment advice.

Risks to ownership:

➤ The risks to owning Growth investments are related to the business-cycle and the ever-changing outlook for the economy or a particular business. The expected return on Growth over time is that we will outpace inflation. The current price is based on future expectations of the company's profits.

Future expectations change minute to minute as new information becomes available. An investor in Growth investments today may believe the price they need to purchase at in order to receive a rate of return over inflation tomorrow is different than the price today.

➤ Another risk that many investors fall victim to is spending countless hours and dollars trying to pick which areas of Growth to invest in and which to avoid. They may pick the wrong areas for Growth, or the wrong companies, but they most often just pay a significant amount in transaction costs, fees, time, and losses for no benefit (Principle #1).

We will cover this topic in greater detail in the implementation section later, but the way to avoid this risk is to invest in one of the two strategies that is not Gambling.

How to invest:

➤ *Institutional class mutual funds.* Mutual funds are a way to own many securities in a cost effective manner. Mutual funds have specific mandates, and so it is important to understand not only the ratings of funds, but whether or not they meet your objectives in a *G/P/S* context. Later we will discuss the difference between institutional class mutual funds and retail mutual funds sold by broker-based financial advisors.

➤ *Globally.* While there are considerations when purchasing a stock whose headquarters resides in a foreign country, the main reason for diversifying globally is that a good company is a good company no matter where they are in the world. With much of the global potential for growth existing outside of our borders, and roughly 60% of the world's economy as well, we have to maintain a global approach to our investment portfolio.

A global approach is especially important as we do not know who will benefit most from a country's growth – the country itself, or foreign companies that provide it with the resources, materials, and services to grow.

Equity Returns of Developed Markets
Annual Return (%)

Boxed Return is highest return for the year

	1986	1987	1988	1989	1990	1991	1992	1993	1994	1995	1996	1997	1998	1999	2000	2001	2002	2003	2004	2005	2006	2007	2008	2009	2010
Australia	42.26	9.25	36.40	9.30	-17.54	33.64	-10.82	36.17	5.40	11.19	16.49	-10.44	6.07	17.62	-9.95	1.68	-1.34	49.46	30.34	16.02	30.86	28.34	-50.67	76.43	14.52
Austria	34.74	2.23	0.57	103.91	6.33	-12.23	-10.65	28.09	-6.28	-4.72	4.51	1.57	0.38	-9.11	-11.96	-5.65	16.55	56.96	71.52	24.64	36.54	2.17	-68.41	43.20	9.98
Belgium	78.37	7.86	53.63	17.29	-10.96	12.77	-1.47	23.51	8.24	25.98	12.03	13.58	67.75	-14.26	-16.85	-10.89	-14.97	35.33	43.53	9.06	38.66	-2.73	-66.48	57.49	-0.42
Canada	9.94	13.91	17.07	24.30	-13.00	11.08	-12.15	17.58	-3.04	18.31	28.54	12.80	-6.14	53.74	5.34	-20.43	-13.19	54.60	22.20	28.31	17.90	29.57	-45.51	56.18	20.45
Denmark	1.24	13.23	52.67	43.94	-0.91	16.66	-28.26	32.91	3.77	18.73	21.79	34.62	8.99	12.06	3.44	-14.81	-16.03	49.28	30.92	24.50	38.77	28.89	-47.86	36.67	30.73
France	79.36	-13.01	37.87	36.15	-13.93	17.63	2.91	20.91	-5.18	14.12	21.20	11.94	41.54	29.27	-4.31	-22.36	-21.16	40.22	18.45	9.88	34.48	13.24	-43.27	31.83	-4.11
Germany	35.29	-24.75	20.80	46.26	-9.36	8.16	-10.27	35.64	4.66	16.41	13.58	24.57	29.43	20.04	-15.59	-22.39	-33.18	63.80	16.17	9.92	38.99	35.21	-45.87	25.16	8.44
Hong Kong	56.11	-4.11	28.12	8.39	9.17	49.52	32.29	116.70	-28.90	22.67	33.08	-23.29	-2.92	59.52	-14.74	-18.61	-17.79	38.10	24.98	8.40	30.38	41.22	-51.21	60.15	23.23
Italy	108.28	-21.30	11.46	19.42	-19.19	-1.82	-22.22	28.53	11.56	1.06	12.59	35.48	52.52	-0.26	-1.33	-26.59	-7.33	37.63	32.49	1.90	32.49	6.06	-49.98	26.57	-15.01
Japan	99.41	43.01	35.39	1.71	-36.10	8.92	-21.45	25.48	21.44	0.69	-15.50	-23.67	5.05	61.53	-28.16	-29.40	-10.28	35.91	15.86	25.52	6.24	-4.23	-29.21	6.25	15.44
Netherlands	40.74	7.07	14.19	35.79	-3.19	17.60	2.30	36.38	11.70	27.71	27.51	23.77	23.23	6.68	-4.09	-22.10	-20.63	28.09	12.24	13.86	31.38	20.59	-48.22	43.25	1.74
Norway	-2.62	5.67	42.40	45.53	0.65	-15.50	-22.29	42.04	23.57	6.02	29.63	6.24	-30.06	31.70	-0.89	-12.23	-7.26	48.11	38.39	24.26	45.12	31.43	-64.24	87.07	10.95
Singapore	48.17	2.28	33.32	42.26	-11.66	24.96	6.29	67.97	6.66	6.45	-6.06	-30.08	-12.88	99.40	-27.72	-23.42	-11.05	37.60	22.27	14.37	46.71	28.35	-47.38	73.96	22.14
Spain	121.29	36.91	13.53	9.76	-13.86	15.63	-21.97	29.75	-4.80	29.83	40.07	25.41	49.90	4.53	-15.86	-11.36	-15.29	58.46	28.93	4.41	49.20	23.95	-40.60	43.48	-21.95
Sweden	65.59	1.99	48.33	31.79	-20.99	14.42	-14.41	36.99	18.34	33.36	37.21	12.92	13.96	79.74	-21.29	-27.13	-30.49	64.53	36.28	10.31	43.39	0.62	-49.98	64.16	33.75
Switzerland	33.37	-9.45	6.18	26.21	-6.23	15.77	17.23	45.79	3.54	44.12	2.28	44.25	23.53	-7.02	5.86	-21.38	-10.31	34.08	14.96	16.33	27.40	5.29	-30.49	25.31	11.79
United Kingdom	26.96	38.09	5.95	21.87	10.29	16.02	-3.66	24.44	-1.63	21.27	27.42	22.62	17.80	12.45	-11.53	-14.06	-15.23	32.06	19.57	7.36	30.61	8.36	-48.34	43.30	8.76
United States	16.26	2.91	14.61	30.21	-3.15	30.07	6.39	9.18	1.13	37.14	23.24	33.38	30.14	21.92	-12.84	-12.39	-23.09	28.41	10.14	5.14	14.67	5.44	-37.57	26.25	14.77

In US dollars.
Source: MSCI developed markets country indices (net dividends) with at least twenty-five years of data. MSCI data copyright MSCI 2011, all rights reserved; see MSCI disclosure page for additional information. Indexes are not available for direct investment. Index performance does not reflect expenses associated with the management of an actual portfolio. Past performance is not a guarantee of future results.

How not to invest:

➤ *Individual stocks.* It is June 2011, and my alma matter's football team, which is regularly picked to finish at the top of national rankings, is embroiled in a scandal that has led to the resignation of the coach, early draft entry of its star quarterback, transfer of key players and recruits, and unknown penalties that may include the loss of future scholarships and a forfeited season.

Six months ago, prior to the scandal becoming public, you would be a fool to have not have picked my former school as a potential winner.

Now, however, it is hard to say if it is a buy, hold, or sell in the football world.

The analogy here holds truth for investing in individual stocks as well. As impossible as it would have been to know this scandal was about to break, consider if you can know the score with an individual company with all of the personalities, motivations, competing internal groups, and so on, in a corporation. No matter what highly paid money managers and advisors will tell you, it just is not possible.

It doesn't matter what your *feelings* are about the company, you cannot know enough to make a decision on the true value outside of what the market price is. On top of that, the risk of owning individual stocks is not compensated; you can expect similar returns, but with a significantly higher degree of risk. The answer is to diversify by owning many companies to protect yourself against individual company risks (Principle #2).

For a further review of the anatomy of one stock-pickers response during the 2008 downturn see *Appendix A – Growth Gurus*.

➤ *Burying risk.* Many investors unknowingly bury their risks by not understanding what their underlying mutual fund investment manager invests in. Even sophisticated investors rarely review the actual holdings of a manager to understand the actual risks they are taking.

Risk and return are related. On the graph below we see that in order to achieve higher returns, managers may add more small companies and "value" companies. There is nothing wrong with this approach, if it is done with intent.

The problem is that investors or advisors who receive additional return have often simply taken more risk they did not mean to. The result is paying a high-cost manager for a simple portfolio change you can make yourself.

Risk and Return Are Related

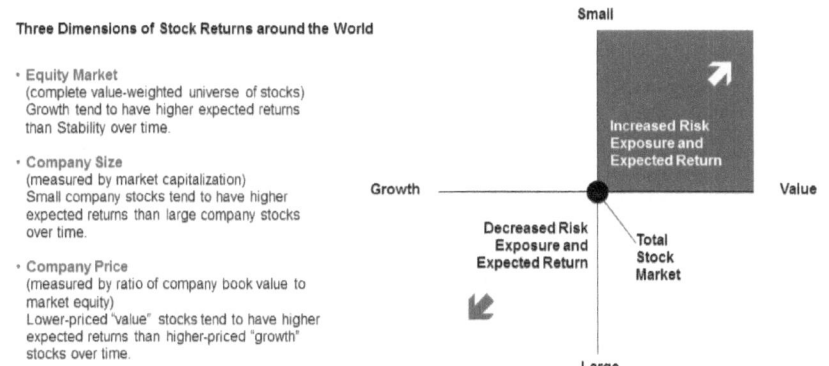

Three Dimensions of Stock Returns around the World

· Equity Market
(complete value-weighted universe of stocks)
Growth tend to have higher expected returns
than Stability over time.

· Company Size
(measured by market capitalization)
Small company stocks tend to have higher
expected returns than large company stocks
over time.

· Company Price
(measured by ratio of company book value to
market equity)
Lower-priced "value" stocks tend to have higher
expected returns than higher-priced "growth"
stocks over time.

➤ *Becoming emotionally involved.* It is easy to become emotionally attached to companies or hot stock fund managers. We 'know' that these companies and funds will continue to do well.

As we will see later, what we think we know about a Growth investment is rarely the case. The market is heartless; it doesn't care whether you need that money for the down payment on a house, or retirement cash flow, or that you know the company you work for is a good investment. Companies have disappeared at no fault of those who believed those were good companies; consider Enron, General Motors (now revived under bankruptcy), Bear Sterns, Lehman Brothers, Washington Mutual, and the list goes on, and on, and on...

Conclusion

The market reacts swiftly and without mercy to new information that enters the pricing conversation. Growth is a long-term proposition, not a short-term gamble like stock pickers would have us believe. When you consider the mindset of making short-term risks with your Growth, it is easy to see how it is gambling, and not investing. A stock's price takes into account information quicker than an analyst can tell you to react. By the time you do, and then settle up with your emotions, it will be far too late.

PRINCIPLES APPLIED TO GROWTH INVESTING:

- ➤ Growth experiences periods of increase and decline.

- ➤ Diversify your Growth globally.

- ➤ Picking stocks or sectors of the stock market individually, or gambling, puts you at risk of great loss.

- ➤ Growth will outperform inflation over the very long term. However, unlike pension funds – where much of our news and investing research originates from – we do not have an infinite time horizon for needing our money. Since we cannot know the periods where Growth will falter, we need Preservation and Stability assets.

Stability

While Preservation fits next in *G / P / S Investing*™ in terms of weighted performance and volatility, it is easier to discuss Preservation after understanding Stability. Stability is the part of long-term investing that dampens the volatile characteristics of Growth, and it is meant to assure income and return of principal.

All investors seek stability, though *what they want is stable Growth!* Since Growth involves significant volatility and risk of loss, Stability provides a measure of safety to portfolios. As there is no such thing as a 'perfect' investment, or one which provides absolute growth with no risk of loss, adding Stability to a portfolio can move a portfolio closer to an ideal investment by limiting losses, while still allowing for some measure of growth.

The types of investments we seek in Stability are the plain, boring, and safe. They are money markets, high quality corporate and government-backed bonds, fixed annuities (though not variable or equity indexed annuities) and other fixed income products. Traditional asset allocation refers to this category as Income, Bonds or Fixed Income. *G / P / S Investing*™ recognizes that not all income investments are created to be safe and stable, that Stability isn't always 'fixed,' and it may not provide income payments all.

Stability for our purposes refers to dollar stability. If you put a dollar into a Stability asset, you have the highest degree of confidence that you will receive a dollar back; or, in the case of a fixed annuity, that you will receive a promise for a fixed future stream of dollars.

Reasons to own:

> ➤ *Provides stability to a portfolio and allows for risk taking in Growth.* Since Growth is volatile, and we may have a need to be able to easily access our money during times where growth can be down in value, it benefits us to have some portion of our money providing stability to the portfolio.
>
> Some advisors prefer to place your Stability investments at risk by investing in high-yield and junk bonds. While the yield on these investments is attractive, the potential to lose makes them as risky as stocks. For that reason (explained in greater detail later) we only recommend investments that meet our goal for stability of principal.
>
> ➤ *To anticipate and cover cash needs.* If you know you need to use money from your portfolio for an upcoming expense, it makes sense to move money to Stability. In retirement this is especially important as you may have regular (or irregular) withdrawal needs from your portfolio. One way to provide for an income stream in retirement is to match your anticipated future withdrawals with an amount in Stability assets that matures at the same time the money is needed.
>
> ➤ *To protect against deflation.* When we experience economic times of deflation, there may also be short-term market setbacks in the

Growth areas of our portfolio, as companies recalibrate their products. While Stability does not earn high rates of return during these periods, it does earn a 'real rate' of return. If prices deflate 10%, stock prices decease to reflect a decrease in profits, but your Stability can now purchase 10% more goods.

➤ *Survive emergency needs for cash.* One of the ways *G / P / S Investing*™ is different than the advice you will see in the media, is that it recognizes that people have emergencies and needs for stable assets in their portfolios. It isn't possible or practical for a Growth money manager to take into account the safety of an individual investor. Stability investments are generally easily exchangeable for cash, without losing much in terms of trading losses or commissions.

The point of Stability is not to keep up with Growth. Stability instead allows us to take risks in Growth, where we have the potential to be rewarded much better.

Risks to ownership:

➤ *Your money will not outpace inflation.* We do not expect to earn a 'real return' in your Stability. This is the case no matter what the yield is. Even in the *good old days* of 10% CDs, inflation eroded those returns to almost nothing. While your lifestyle costs rise, the money you place into Stability will not grow at a similar pace, and so you will experience a slow decline in purchasing power.

You are protected from inflation in the Growth and Preservation parts of your portfolio. In a way, Stability protects you from monetary deflation.

➤ *Reaching for yield.* It can be difficult to look at Stability assets without wanting to reach for just a little more yield. But increasing your investment by not even one half percent more can put what you thought to be safe money at risk. I provide a few examples later, but it is important to realize that Stability only works when it provides dollar safety and it doesn't provide dollar safety when it is at risk.

Several famous investors have commented that: **More money has been lost chasing yield (i.e., seeking a higher yield on Stability) then has been lost at the point of a gun.**

How to invest:

- ➤ *FDIC or NCUA Insured accounts.* Money markets, savings, and traditional CDs (not equity-linked or other types of CDs) are acceptable substitutes for bonds generally for money needed in four years or less.

- ➤ *Institutional class mutual funds.* When researching bond mutual funds it is important to understand more than a rating and how the fund has performed in the past. Bond funds that outperform their index often hold risky securities as well as derivative investments that can have significant risk.

  Consider if you are a Stability investment manager and your fund only buys a specific type of bond (1-5 year U.S. Government Treasury bonds). There is not much that you can do to standout from other managers in a similar category. Your choices are to take on more risk to earn a higher return, or put your bonds at risk with a derivative. As such, many fund managers add risk to show better performance than their peers, but adding risk isn't rewarded in bonds; it is rewarded in Growth.

- ➤ *Individual bonds.* You can cut out the middle man and purchase individual bonds, but I only recommend this when buying the high quality government bonds, and when you have a specific spending purpose for the bond (e.g., you will need $50,000 in 2 years for the down payment on a house). The type of bonds you purchase will depend on asset location, tax rate, and other factors, however, you should stick to the highest quality bonds, as it never pays to risk your fixed income.

- ➤ *Globally.* Some advisors argue against investing globally for fixed income because of costs and fluctuating exchange rates.

Investing globally does not mean investing in risky countries or corporations. Instead of Gambling or Indexing, we can be selective about owning the market by excluding bonds that do not represent good long-term investments, and monitoring the portfolio to make sure our holdings maintain their quality.

Hedging our bonds to the foreign currency, we can diversify and minimize currency risk. This does add cost, but just as diversifying into foreign stocks reduces risk, adding the uncorrelated aspect of high-quality foreign bond yields to the U.S. yields can add stability and excess return to a portfolio. We also recommend an unhedged position to a portion of your bonds as a Preservation investment, described more in the next section.

PRINCIPLES APPLIED TO STABILITY INVESTING:

➤ Globally diversify your Stability assets.

➤ Stability assets have no real return over time.

➤ The purpose of Stability is to provide for shorter-term future liabilities (known or unknown), and to allow for risk taking with a portion of the portfolio.

➤ Longer-term Stability, like annuities, places the stable portion of your portfolio at high risk of being diminished by inflation.

➤ Reaching for just a little more yield in Stability is not worth the risk. Risk is better compensated in Growth assets.

Preservation

Preservation in simple terms is investing with the goal of maintaining the 'real value,' or purchasing power, of your money. Because some in the finance world argue that it isn't a true investment, this section is a little more detailed to explain why holding Preservation in a portfolio can provide benefits to an individual's portfolio.

Preservation involves owning what are known as Real Assets: Real Estate, Commodities, Materials, Gold, Silver, and other types of assets that are meant to keep pace with inflation.

Reasons to own:

> ➤ *Diversification from stocks and bonds.* There are economic situations when both stocks and bonds suffer, where various types of Preservation may not.

> ➤ *Reduce volatility in your portfolio.* Over longer time periods, holding Preservation assets has been shown to dampen the volatility of a portfolio without decreasing returns. Over shorter time periods it may even increase returns.

Do you need to own Preservation investments? Many argue they are not necessary. However, let me dive just a little deeper into the reasoning for including Preservation in portfolio design.

While not entirely new, this is still considered by some advisors to be a 'new' frontier in investing. Many professionals apply the term 'alternatives' for this group. A lot of that has to do with these individual professional's view of these assets compared to traditional financial assets such as stocks and bonds.

The Finance Argument

The finance argument states that many real assets have no long-term investment value. They either increase less than Growth, or, as in the case of commodities substitutes may take the place of an expensive commodity. This view claims that Growth and Stability are enough for a diversified portfolio.

Someone who practices a textbook approach to finance would argue that if you own the actual stocks, you participate in the rise in the price of an asset by owning the company, more so than the commodity. This belief is that your Stability assets provide enough protection from volatile stocks.

In general, the above is true. You are probably covered over an investment cycle (10-20 years) if you just own Growth in combination with Stability.

Where the problem lies is that in order to experience those gains, you may have to hold your stocks for a very, very long time. The finance argument makes perfect sense for those with unlimited timeframes. Individuals however simply do not have the time pension funds have to recover from a downturn.

From an economic standpoint, Stability assets have over the last 100 years mostly been acceptable over the short to mid-term at covering the goals of both Stability and Preservation. We have grown used to a small amount of inflation, and deflation in areas like consumer goods, and have placed more value on the 'safety' of dollar stability over purchasing power preservation.

However, Stability is not Preservation. Preservation accepts that other assets can be equally or more efficient as dollars or government bonds at protecting purchasing power. Preservation can be practically owned in various ways in today's financial instruments, and so we recommend an allocation to these assets, as a part of a balanced portfolio.

The Economic Argument for Preservation Investments

Money has several purposes. It is a unit of account and a way to transact with others. Money is also a 'store of value.' Meaning that a dollar today is not only worth a dollar tomorrow, but there is the assumption that it should buy *a dollar's worth of yesterdays goods* <u>for</u> *a dollar tomorrow.*

That idea has always seemed to me to be one of those academic assumptions you learn in school that logically makes sense, but just doesn't fit into how the real world actually operates. It has a very similar feeling to other economic theories, where we start with an assumption that everyone *always* acts in their best economic interest to achieve their maximum utility.

However, we don't always act that way! Otherwise, there wouldn't be a need for financial advisors (or for this book!).

An Ever Changing World

The investing and economic climate is ever changing. People have sought preservation in many ways. Years ago, savers put their money into cattle to preserve its value. Cattle represented a need; like money it could be used, barter for other goods, or sold for a profit. Throughout history, animals, crops, real estate, and other real things have been places to preserve value. Though, like Growth, Preservation is not without its share of bubbles and bumps in the road.

Lately (over the last several decades), we have grown accustomed to expecting 2-4% inflation, and simply accept that as a part of our Stability. If we buy a long-term bond, we have what is known as an 'inflation expectation' built into the return (or yield) that we want. If we want to earn 2% on our money, we may ask for a return of 5 or 6% to account for inflation. President George W. Bush was famously mocked when he said that a 2% return on a bond was a good return, though in some sense he wasn't far off. Depending on the bond, a 2% 'real return' (2% above the inflation rate) is normal, and may even been good.

In recent years we have used another asset to keep the value of our dollar – our homes. Part of the reasoning that many bought houses, or made large improvements on their current home, was that they thought of it as "an investment." What they meant was, in their mind, placing the money in the home has multiple benefits past simply being able to enjoy the new home, addition, or improvement. Part of that belief was that their choice to place their dollars into a home will not only increase the value of their home today, but also when they choose to sell. They expected that their $25,000 will at least be *preserved* with respect to the purchasing power it will have when they want to call on it in the future.

And though we had a bubble in housing, over time people will put their money into Real Assets that they see as having the opportunity to grow their money at a higher rate than Stability.

You can see that in some ways Preservation is similar to Stability. Prior to the 20th century we had a period in our history where we didn't worry about buying power. Innovation forced the price of goods down and we see that idea still holds true in many ways today. Our computers and cell phones are much faster, more advanced, and cost a fraction of what the original cost. Preservation may not be absolutely necessary, but in a world where we continue to debase the value of our dollar, at potentially an increasing rate to cover our unfunded obligations, it may be that Preservation in many ways protects our spending power better than Stability.

People, rightly or wrongly, will do what they think is best to preserve the value of their dollars, which is in many ways the value of their past labors. For that reason, we use Preservation assets as a complement to Stability and as a diversifier to Growth.

Risks to own:

> ➤ *Preservation assets can be volatile.* However, in combination with an already diverse portfolio, that volatility can provide a more stable portfolio, compared to a portfolio without.

> ➤ *Preservation may not be perfectly correlated with inflation statistics, and the investment vehicles may not provide a return equal to a specific asset.* The returns on Preservation investments will not match a specific benchmark for inflation like the Consumer Price Index.

> There are many reasons for this. Partially it speaks to how our government calculates inflation. Mainly it is simply a function of what we can buy. Inflation calculations vary widely, even within different government measurements. Alternate approaches suggest inflation is tied to the amount of money produced, but again, this and any other measures are not perfectly correlated to inflation statistics.

➤ *You may not earn 'inflation' type returns.* Since there are competing definitions of inflation, and because it is impossible to own an index or a formula, we do not see the inflation correlation as a reason to not own Preservation. Some advisors view this as a reason not to own Preservation, but we can note that neither Growth nor Stability assets have a similar requirement to meet a predetermined return. Model calculations of inflation may never be available to receive in an investment form, and it probably should not.

➤ *Preservation investing can include costs for storing goods, and costs of financial products.* Certain investments may not involve owning an asset itself, but a financial contract. These ideas are outside the scope of this book, but it is important to realize an investor may experience different returns than outright owning certain types of Preservation assets.

How to invest:

➤ *Mutual funds, exchange-traded funds, and REITs.* Preservation asset classes can be owned through simple financial products. Real Estate in the United States is owned through Real Estate Investment Trusts (REITs). Publicly-traded REITs are exchanged on stock markets just like stocks. The difference between a REIT and a stock is that a REIT has to pay out to investors by law almost all of the income it receives from its real estate operations, whereas stocks have no such rule. It acts as a pass-through entity for you to be a real estate manager.

Through mutual funds or exchange-traded funds, you can own a diversified basket of REITs and other Preservation assets such as precious metals, commodities, and inflation-protected bonds.

➤ *Global real estate.* They are not just not making more real estate. As land is put into higher production uses all over the world, its value increases. Since there is a high potential for transforming land from being unproductive to highly productive in foreign countries, it only makes sense that we continue our belief in global investing in our real estate holdings.

➤ *Direct ownership.* Gold, silver, and many commodities can be held directly in coins, bars, etc. Direct ownership has high transaction and storage fees, and is not easy to convert to dollars at a known cost.

How not to invest:

➤ *A basement full of perishables; burying gold in the backyard.* Many who buy gold do so with a doomsday, or an end of the world mindset.

There is no reason to have to worry about having physical assets that can be stolen. Keep your finances separate from your home life to the extent possible. Even when expecting the worst. Short-term emergencies are the reason to have Preservation assets as a part of your portfolio, not gold coins.

If, however, the financial markets and political stability in the U.S. finally comes to an end, it won't matter how much gold you have in the backyard. All the gold in the world won't buy food or other necessities.

➤ *A gold company you saw on T.V.* Many of these companies are giving used car dealers a good name (I don't have anything against used car dealers, but they may be glad for public perception purposes to know what gold companies are up to).

Thanks to the internet, many of these firms have been investigated by other gold experts and found to have been ripping off their customers – from the classic bait-and-switch techniques, to simply delivering their products at an incredible markup compared to their competition. Be very inquisitive about who you choose to do business with if you own gold direct. For this and other reasons it is often best to own through an investment fund.

The following products are sold by advisors who are also brokers. They have a few similar characteristics that make them poor products for individual investors. All have high costs, high commissions, no public market (no way to get out at a reasonable price, or to rebalance), and have had questionable and sometimes *self-reported* results. Most products allow the product sponsor to share in the gain, sometimes with a guarantee of gain prior to sharing a return with the investors who risked their money. Many times this means the promoter takes a gain that you would consider very reasonable for risking your money… but why risk *their* money, when they can gamble with *yours?*

➤ *Managed futures.* Broker-advisors for many years have recommended managed futures as a way to invest in commodities. In addition to the problems listed above, the reported returns of these products have been called into question by historically being both 'self-reported' by the investment managers, and excluding many funds that fail (some estimate ~15-20% of funds fail annually).

Jason Zweig, personal finance writer for The Wall Street Journal, has noted that the costs of managed futures funds can include 6-8% of expenses for the investment manager per year.

Consider that we may only expect these funds to keep up with inflation. Now subtract 6-8% of what you expect these funds to achieve. It is likely you would be better off placing the money in a low-yielding bank account over investing in a product with these types of costs.

➤ *Private REITs.* These versions of REITs are sold direct to investors rather than over the stock market. While many variations exist, they mainly seek to purchase real estate properties, bundle them into a portfolio, and then sell that portfolio after a holding period. They hope to either earn income from rents, or appreciation on the properties.

Here in 2011 there is a significant amount of uncertainty and litigation[i] over private REITs who both did not adequately price their products, and sold their illiquid offerings to people who needed access to their money.

A wholesaler of these products once told me a story about a competitors experience with an offering they made to the general public. He ended the story with the comment that *the retail investor always gets ripped-off in private real estate.*

Do you have any reason to believe he was lying? **I don't.** Though I don't believe he intended me to equate his story to his firm. He just meant every other retail, private REIT ripped-off investors. Not his company I'm certain.

Private REITs often run REITS for pension funds and institutional clients, in addition to their retail offerings. I've always been curious at the selection process of properties for these offerings; how do they know which properties are worthy of their valued pension fund relationships versus their retail customers?

As noted above, there is no public market for private REITs, and so you will not be able to sell your interests at a reasonable price to another investor. Illiquid investments also can impact your rebalancing decision making. You will have no say about when you receive your money back, and the distribution phase can last many years.

➤ *Oil and natural gas wells.* These broker advisor sold investments are far too risky for the average multi-millionaire investor. *Note: I say this with sarcasm, realizing many of my readers will not be of this status, but may themselves be presented with these investment pitches. In truth, I wouldn't recommend these products to any client, no matter their net worth.*

A sales feature of these items has been a tax deduction for a significant portion of the investment. As we know, tax deductions can change, and this one has been discussed frequently by legislators as a 'loophole' that should be closed. When you invest in these products, expect to be treated by future legislators as a *rich* investor who is benefiting from a tax loophole that needs to be closed.

Another feature of the tax deduction is that in order to receive it, you must open yourself up to personal liability for what happens at the well.

I once worked for an advisor who sold these products rather heavily. Even with the tax break, after 5, 10, and 15 years I did not see one client who was happy with the low and diminishing cash flow from their wells. None were happy with the rate of return of their money, and few received their initial investment back, even after nearly a decade. There is no public market to trade oil wells on, and so you are in this investment for the long-run, even when it turns out poorly.

➤ *Equipment leasing.* These partnerships are basically the same as above. You need to keep in mind the long leasing terms, and how we live in a world where tools and technology are changing in shorter and shorter periods. At the end of the program, you have to hope you can sell your equipment at a reasonable price.

The following is a story I once heard from a fund manager that summarizes how the broker advisor sold investment arraignments work when it comes to two aspects: the **Money** and the **Experience**.

To start, many of the above types of investment programs bring in a General Partner (the person who runs the partnership) who has great **experience** in the given industry. You, the investor, brings the **money** that he will manage.

After the investment has run its course, the General Partner leaves the relationship with the **money** he has earned and a generous share of the profits (sometimes this is a guaranteed share of profits prior to the investor receiving a dime), and meanwhile all that you have for investing is <u>an **experience** you will never want to repeat again!</u>

PRINCIPLES APPLIED TO PRESERVATION INVESTING:

➤ Preservation is the attempt to maintain the purchasing power of your dollar by owning assets that should increase in value with inflation.

➤ Inflation happens to assets at different rates, and calculations of inflation as it relates to your personal increases in cost of living are not possible. Therefore, owning a diverse basket of Preservation assets is recommended.

➤ Broker-advisor sold products in this area are often not worth the cost, lack of diversification, or inaccessibility to your money.

➤ True Stability has a dual meaning – keeping the dollars that you have AND keeping the buying power of those dollars. Therefore a mix of Preservation with Stability is appropriate.

➤ The 'real return' of an investment (the return above inflation) is what counts.

The Investment Mix

Allocate Your Money

The investment mix is known as your asset allocation. It is how you divide your money between the *G / P / S* categories. It is also how you make decisions in each of the groups on how to further divide that money into sub-asset allocations.

Determining the investment mix is a critical piece of how you will perform as an investor. In fact, it is likely to be the decision that accounts for the greatest amount of the returns you achieve. More so than picking the right mutual fund, hot stock, or guessing where the market will go in the next day, week, month or year.

The main decisions in how to allocate your investment dollars are:

➤ How much money do we risk into growth investments?

➤ How much lost long-term growth opportunity do we risk with preservation investments that provide shorter-term protection? And,

➤ How much purchasing power do we risk with stable investments?

Your asset allocation will determine the majority of your performance as an investor. Due to its level of important, it is critical to work with an advisor who reviews your asset allocation in terms of two items: your tolerance for risk, and your goals. Only a minor portion of your returns will come from short-term gambling, which as often as not gives a random result.

Structure Determines Performance

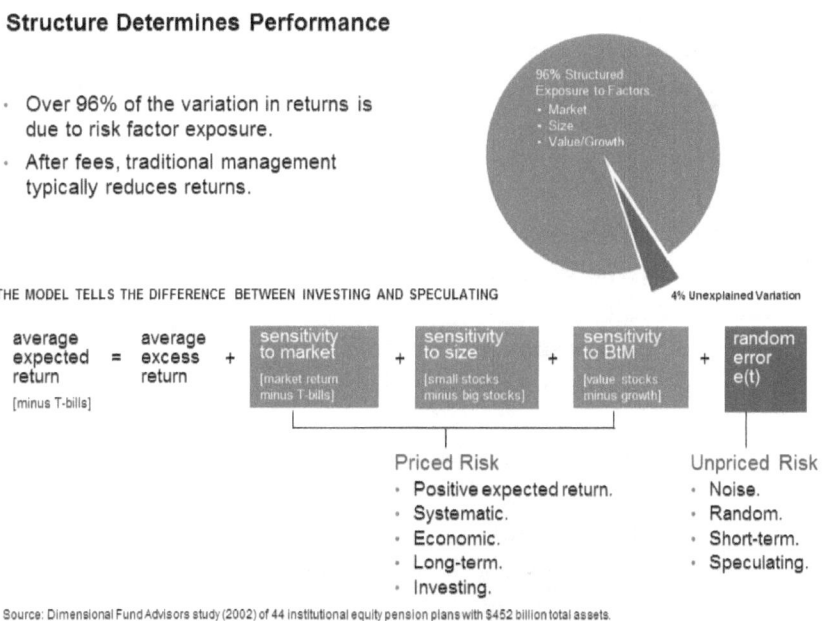

- Over 96% of the variation in returns is due to risk factor exposure.
- After fees, traditional management typically reduces returns.

96% Structured Exposure to Factors.
- Market
- Size
- Value/Growth

THE MODEL TELLS THE DIFFERENCE BETWEEN INVESTING AND SPECULATING

4% Unexplained Variation

average expected return [minus T-bills] = average excess return + sensitivity to market [market return minus T-bills] + sensitivity to size [small stocks minus big stocks] + sensitivity to BtM [value stocks minus growth] + random error e(t)

Priced Risk
- Positive expected return.
- Systematic.
- Economic.
- Long-term.
- Investing.

Unpriced Risk
- Noise.
- Random.
- Short-term.
- Speculating.

Source: Dimensional Fund Advisors study (2002) of 44 institutional equity pension plans with $452 billion total assets. Factor analysis run over various time periods, averaging nine years. Total assets based on total plan dollar amounts as of year end 2001. Average explanatory power (R²) is for the Fama/French equity benchmark universe.

How to Protect from a Bubble

After two major bubbles in the last decade – the tech / internet bubble and the housing bubble – we are all sensitive about investing into a bubble.

For many, that has made them swear off all markets, and keep their money in safe and Stable assets.

Bubbles can and do happen in any sector. Many do not realize it, but Stability can be subject to a bubble as well. When investors are fearful, they flock to stable investments, driving their prices up, and the yields of safe investments down. This driving down of yields is a characteristic of a Stability bubble, where there is too much money in bank accounts, bonds, and safe assets, and because of that, banks do not have to pay much in order to attract assets.

Ways to protect against a bubble

> ➤ *Diversify not only over Growth / Preservation / Stability, but also diversify within each.* Sometimes a bubble develops in one area of the market. During the run-up to the year 2000 bust, large technology stocks ran rampant, and everyone wanted in on the action. When that bubble burst, many rode the rollercoaster down well below where they bought in.
>
> Meanwhile, an investor with a balanced allocation over all stocks, Stability and Preservation didn't fare nearly as badly. While large stocks had negative returns for 2000, 2001, and 2002, small stocks bounced back strong in 2001. Investors in real estate stocks were likely up all three years.
>
> Over the so-called 'lost decade' of 2000 to 2010, large cap stocks (as measured by the S&P 500) lost money. However, a diverse portfolio with small stocks, international, international small, emerging markets, and Preservation assets would have a positive return, with many of the indexes of the alternate asset groups earning 6-12% per year over the same period.
>
> ➤ *Set targets to monitor your investments.* To monitor your investments, set a target allocation for each asset class. Setting targets will help you avoid becoming a Gambler (we will discuss Gambling shortly).
>
> ➤ *Rebalance when your investments are too far out of target.* When you set a target allocation for each investment you make an intentional

decision not be emotional. You will be less likely to buy into the bubble, and when you rebalance to your target you will have established a prudent investment strategy of selling an asset that has increased at a faster rate than other. You buy when an asset is relatively low, and sell when it is relatively high – *which is the key to investment success!*

There are many studies that discuss how to rebalance in the best way. The short answer is what has worked best depends on the time period analyzed. We utilize a combination approach, reviewing portfolios regularly and rebalancing when a trigger point is reached. There isn't anything particularly magical about what trigger point or timeframe you may select to rebalance, except that it should be sure to consider transaction costs and taxes.

A successful asset allocation involves setting realistic targets, not changing your targets to accommodate asset bubbles, and rebalancing with a method that takes into account transaction costs.

Asset Location

Not only is asset allocation important, but as an investor you should also consider what investments you will hold in the various types of accounts you have, or else you may pay unnecessarily in taxes.

Many money manager advisors give little credence to what is known as 'asset location.' This approach is done for their benefit to make it simple to rebalance all clients with a computer program. They may place you with a Moderate Growth portfolio strategy of funds in each of your accounts with them. By utilizing this approach you are not taking advantage of the specific tax attributes of investments and the different tax-advantaged accounts that you may have.

For example, many Stability and Preservation assets have characteristics that make them ideal for holding in a tax-advantaged account such as an IRA,

401(k), or 403(b). Likewise, it may make sense to use tax-efficient Growth in taxable accounts. Growth investments with very high expected returns often makes sense to place into Roth accounts such as Roth IRAs or workplace plans such as a Roth 403(b) and Roth 401(k).

Goals and Risk Tolerance

It's important to stop when diving into the workings of money and investments to realize our main objective is to learn how to invest to meet our goals. Our goal isn't to find the latest Wall Street product that will give you a leg up on your neighbors, be able to improve your skills at stock picking, or in any way be a race to 'beat' the markets. Investing is personal to your goals and needs for growth. Without goals, you are preparing to take a trip *without anywhere to go*.

In order to help pick the proper allocation, it also is important to consider both your risk tolerance. You may be familiar with the term risk tolerance; it describes an idea that investors can measure their comfort with risk in some way.

Think of risk tolerance as a measurement of your pain threshold – it is how much market pain you believe you can endure. While it is important to understand the concept, it is not the only, or even the main consideration in determining your asset allocation. In addition to knowing your pain tolerance level, I believe what is of greater personal importance to most individuals is the question:

How much pain do I need to expose myself to?

This question makes us consider the asset allocation question in the context of an intentional investing methodology. Rather than simply investing based on pain threshold, we purposefully discuss retirement needs to view the amount of pain we need to be exposed to. With that knowledge, a discussion can be had on how much market exposure is necessary, and does it fit within your risk tolerance. If so, then the asset allocation decision can be determined from the minimum amount of market exposure necessary. If not, then a conversation with your advisor should be had on if it is more important to bear the increased risks in the market, lower your financial goals, or try to meet them by a different path.

Consider too that you may be willing to lower a goal before increasing your investment risk. This is a personal decision, and requires having a more personal conversation about your goals with your advisor than simply reviewing a risk tolerance test.

Implementing Your Plan

The above are the basics. They give us a starting point for how to think about the portfolio model that fits our lives.

But, models are always different than building the real world plan. You have a number of different accounts to coordinate your plan over, or you may have products in your plan today that you are not sure fit into a $G / P / S$ strategy.

So, how do you effectively implement your portfolio plan to consider asset allocation, asset location, risk tolerance, and your goals, and also stay true to $G / P / S$ principles?

The following section deals with how to implement a successful investment plan, as well as the pitfalls to look out for along the way.

Intentional Investing

Pulling Together the Pieces

The beauty of personal financial planning is that it is personal. There are no magic bullets, crystal balls, or individual answers that will work best for everyone. While the principles are the same, and parts of a plan will always rely on universally accepted standards, all plans require personalization to fit **your** uniqueness.

While many investors make it to this point with their plan, it is the in the implementation stage where the wheels start to come off of an otherwise sound investment strategy. If you do not understand which of the three ways your advisor is implementing your plan, and the ramifications of each, you could find your plan taken off track.

The Three Implementation Options

Boiling down the world of investment strategies, there are actually only three implementation choices you (or your advisor) can make. The majority of advisors you will find work in the Gambling arena, and after reading this I hope you will have the tools to determine if this method of investing actually is intentionally attempting to meet your goals.

Gamble

As discussed earlier, Gambling is taking risks with your money to seek outsized gains, but tends to ignore risks. We'll discuss specific Gambling methods later, but terms like active management or tactical asset allocation, are two common methods of gambling. In this section it is important to realize the difference between gambling and investing, and spot where you may have a Gambling approach in your portfolio.

My largest beef with Gambling is that it unconsciously teaches us that the activity of investing is literally a gamble. It reduces the concept of investing to the extremes: by assuming you are willing to take outsized risks to bet on outsized gains, or ignore volatility and gamble that inflation won't be an issue with low-rate investments.

Most investors I meet with are seeking a more rational plan; presumably one based on scientific evidence, and one that considers their financial goals and plans. What happens in the implementation stage of most plans is you are presented with options that follow neither evidence or the plan itself. You are attacked with a Gambling sales pitch on an emotional level for an activity you believed would be a professional service, but ends up little more than a wager.

If you think of the stock market and have the same feeling of risk as you would with placing a bet on a horse at the track, then your advisor is not giving you the information you need to know the difference between a long-term wealth building strategy, and one where you could lose your money instantly.

It is true that placing all of your money on XYZ Company, or say on the Detroit Red Wings to win the Stanley Cup would both be gambles. And let me also suggest that the same reason people place bets on an individual sports team is the same reason they purchase individual stocks. Feelings. Emotional attachments. The thrill of winning.

None of the above is what you should hire an advisor for, or expect in an investing plan. In sports, the true investors are the owners. The owners win no matter what happens to the Gamblers. And yet, most strategies implemented by advisors and advocated by the mass media are Gambling strategies as opposed to ownership investing.

When individuals think in gambling terms, it is easy to understand why there are many nervous investors in the markets. They don't see that a balanced *G / P / S* investment strategy builds long-term wealth and seeks to minimize risks, because they have the mindset of a Gambler.

But, we can know that Gambling is a fraud when we weigh its validity in contrast to the principles of investing. Let's review each of the principles we discussed earlier, and see how Gambling compares:

> **Principle #1: The financial markets work.** A gambler's first goal will be to convince you that markets do not work. There is a loophole they discovered that the millions of other eyes on the markets haven't yet found.
>
> To believe this, one must believe that an idea that 'beats the market' can be turned into a product, marketed, sold to investors, invested in for decades, and all the while it maintains its ability to continue to exploit those same opportunities with no one else catching on. Not likely.

> **Principle #2: Diversification is critical.** This principle too is thrown out the window by Gamblers. You need a stock picker's 'best idea' stocks, and that's all. Jim Cramer, a celebrity stock-picker, has a segment in his T.V. show titled '*Am I Diversified?*' where callers present five stocks and Cramer tells them if they have enough diversification. According to every academic study on the topic the answer is five stocks does not diversify enough to remove the risks of individual stock holding but no one ever said Gambling relies on academic research.

> **Principle #3: If you want more return, you need to take more risk.** Gamblers always try to convince you that a financial product or strategy, will provide you more for less. *They* will give you stock-like returns, without the risk. *They* will protect your portfolio and give you growth, again, without the risk. I analyze these products on a regular basis, and consistently find that Gamblers do not come near to their promised returns, to the significant detriment of their investors. Remember the graph at the beginning of the book of the results of an increase in costs? Many of these products hide their costs, and risks, but the true cost is the significantly lower portfolio at retirement.

➤ **Principle #4: How you structure your portfolio explains your performance.** Gamblers pay little credence to the structure of a portfolio. While they may discuss a portfolio in the context of a financial plan, this is an illusion, generally done simply to allow them to make their pitch for a "better" investment product. As we noted earlier, this is the same as throwing your grocery list and map out the window. The end result of the portfolio is the same as it would have been without the plan, making the plan simply a sales tool.

In addition, we know that investing differs from gambling because Gambling does not minimize risks. It may pay lip service to reducing risks in the vein that above average returns will be had, but all the Gambler does is attempt to take your critical mind off of considering the risks. They tend to sell ideas rather than discuss how poorly the investment managers they previously recommended performed.

Gamblers simply accept that a risk of total loss always exists, and are willing to take that bet (with your money). Intentional investors on the other hand recognize that their capital grows when invested wisely, according to principles, and risks we mean to take.

Probably the worst part about gambling, is it takes the financial game plan, throws it in the trash, and then puts your money into an unintentional portfolio based nothing on what your plan analyzed.

You have a financial plan. You project out a scenario, based on specific anticipated returns and risks, and then discuss how a certain product actually protects you better than what your plan calls for, while providing all of the returns of the market.

Gambling doesn't pay

OK, you still may not convinced about the lack of value in actively guessing what funds or stocks will do better than others. If you are, feel free to skip ahead to the Price-Taking investment style section. But, if you need further proof, may be susceptible to a good sales pitch, or think you may be working with an advisor who is a Gambler, read on.

What does it take to beat the market?

1) **Luck**

Studies have found that mutual fund managers performance can be attributed more to luck than any skill at beating the markets.

One study by Russ Wermers of the University of Maryland at College Park found that over a 32 year period 24% of active fund managers were 'unskilled,' meaning their stock picking after costs did harm to investor returns. 75.4% of managers were neither skilled or unskilled; they did not provide any excess returns to investors after their costs were taken into account.

I can hear you saying to yourself now... 24% plus 75% equals...

Yes, the remaining 0.6% of funds were the stock market gurus who could claim that they have produced their results on the basis of skill. This study did not take into account investment fees including advisor fees that one would have to pay to select these managers.

What it means is you most likely will not have a manager who intentionally outperforms the market. If you choose to Gamble, you have to pay for the right to simply have a mediocre investment. A normal Gambler fund can cost between 1.00% and 1.75% before advisor fees and other investor transaction costs.

How difficult is it to Gamble? Just take a look at what happens if managers miss out on the top 10% of performers in a given year... your return drops by 35%. And if they miss the top 25%? The average return of your manager would drop from an average return of 9.7% of all U.S. stocks from 1926-2010, to a negative 0.5%.

Missing Opportunity

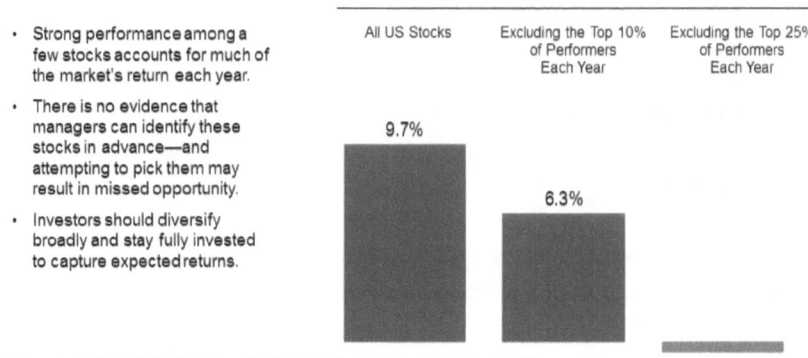

Compound Average Annual Returns: 1926-2010

- Strong performance among a few stocks accounts for much of the market's return each year.

- There is no evidence that managers can identify these stocks in advance—and attempting to pick them may result in missed opportunity.

- Investors should diversify broadly and stay fully invested to capture expected returns.

Results based on the CRSP 1-10 Index. CRSP data provided by the Center for Research in Security Prices, University of Chicago.

When your fund manager only invests in their 'highest conviction' stocks, or a dozen or more out of several thousand available, what do you believe are the chances they miss the top 10 or 25%?

2)   **Investing unintentionally**

Managers that outperform most often do so by investing outside of the area you hire them for. If you hire a large company manager, they often will seek greater returns taking more risk by adding small company or emerging markets stocks to a portfolio. And while diversification is preferred, what we want is intentional diversification, not random diversification.

This occurrence is known as *style drift*. The manager invests outside of the intended style, and gambles to gather more return. Meanwhile, your portfolio may be at higher risk as the manager is now investing in a style where you may already have sufficient money allocated, and he is duplicating your efforts.

On top of your mutual fund manager adding risk, your investment advisor may allocate your funds to managers based only on past performance. Past performance is often higher because the manager took more risk. If your financial advisor is also a gambler, she is doubling down on risk when gambling with gamblers.

If your advisor only picks funds based on performance or mutual fund ratings, as is the norm, then they are probably adding risk to your portfolio, not investing according to plan, and opting you in for a riskier path than maybe necessary.

3)   Their hands are tied

While you, the investor, wants to be able to compare this manger to an index, or a star rating, doing so ties your managers hands. They are heavily influenced in their decision making to not change the portfolio too much so that they will be placed in another category. They do not want to lose to the index, and so they will likely invest almost identical to it – it is better for ratings (and therefore business) to not take the chances they may want, or limit chances, and invest primarily just like the index. But, since Gamblers cost significantly more, you don't receive the full benefit of their expertise when they are being tied to an index.

4)   To do what very few have done

In an effort to not appear to dislike Gamblers (I don't dislike them, really, I just don't think they make sense as managers of money for people), let me share that I do think it is possible that individuals exist who possess talent to beat the markets.

The problem is you can't hire them.

Nonsense you say? Of course they can be hired, you think?

Yes, they may be able to be hired. Just not by you.

Think about it. If you had the skill to beat the markets, on a consistent basis, would you share your secret with the world where it would be duplicated until there was no value that could be gained from it?

Consider the following manager, neighbor, or other person who claims to have the way to beat the market.

Without telling anyone, one skilled manager may be able to earn a high excess returns. Maybe they find a niche to exploit in the markets where they had luck implementing a strategy for a few months.

Now, they tell you, and you see the merits and start to implement the plan. You and the market guru now gain from the strategy, but you earn slightly less because you both are bidding for the same investments. With more buyers, the competition increases, as does the price. When the price is higher, the expected profits to exploit the niche are lower.

Later, you tell your siblings, partner, parents, and BFFs. They all see the merits of the strategy and invest along with you.

As you think back, you realize all of the people you told have told others. The strategy continues to work, for a time, but you notice that your returns are lessened. More and more people are diluting your returns.

And this is what happens with every Gambler, whether they are a mutual fund manager, hedge fund guru, or well-meaning uncle.

I would guess there are a handful of people who could do this job successfully as the strategy grows, and they have to develop new strategies to maintain the same level of return. And since they quickly would reach a level where only billionaires can afford their services, forgetting the high fees you will have to pay them, forgetting the fact that they have to be luckier than 99% of other Gamblers... is it worth throwing away your time in an attempt to find this person?

It is also important to realize that the best-of-the-best gamblers believe that the best plan for the average multi-millionaire—or multi-millionaire in training—is to invest intentionally and to *NOT* gamble. Below are just a few examples.

David Swensen, Chief Investment Officer of Yale's pension fund, whose success is frequently cited by gamblers as proof gambling works. Swensen sought to write a book on the ways the average investor could implement a Gambling strategy profitably. His conclusion? *They should not even try.*

Brokers frequently ignore Swensen's own conclusions and try to convince investors they can help you "invest like Yale." To my mind the most frightening aspect is the fact Gamblers are so arrogant in their sales pitch that do not even know Yale's opinion on the subject! If this isn't a telling sign for how little research some Gambler's actually do, then I don't know what is.

Peter Lynch, ex-manager of the highly successful Fidelity Magellan fund admitted that:

"All the time and effort that people devote to picking the right fund, the hot hand, the great manager, have in most cases led to no advantage."

While Mr. Lynch was one of the most prominent gamblers in mutual fund history, he was unable to pick a manager to succeed him who could continue his success. His hand-picked successors led to the failure of the fund, and significant losses to its investors.

Since the best-of-the-best gamblers not appear to have the skill to find other skilled gamblers, how can we be certain we can either?

Survival Rates

Need more proof that outperformance is due to risk and taking too much risk? Let's see who not only performs at a high level for a few years, but who survives after five years.

The following chart shows the performance of the top performing mutual funds of 2001-2005. Of the top funds, only 19% stayed within the top category. Another 14% would have put you in the top 50% of funds.

Subsequent Performance of Top 25% of US Equity Funds
As of December 31, 2010

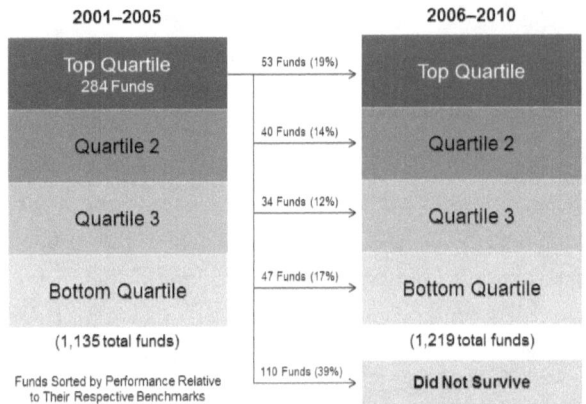

The left column represents all US equity funds in the CRSP Mutual Fund Database with a complete return history for 2001–2005. The funds are sorted by performance relative to their benchmarks. Funds in the top quartile are then tracked and directed to their subsequent performance quartiles in the following 5-year period (2006–2010), or to the "Did Not Survive" category. Quartiles in the following period reflect all funds with a complete return history. Percentages may not total 100% due to rounding.

Source: CRSP Survivor-Bias-Free US Mutual Fund Database.

What was the most likely outcome? Your fund was disbanded. Why? The most common reason a fund is closed is horrendous performance.

After all of the research, all of the time spent reading up on the top funds, all of the recommendations from the financial press about *the funds you need to own today...* you had:

➤ A greater than 1/3 chance that the performance was so bad that it would no longer exist;

➤ A better than 2/3 chance that your fund selection would have performed worse than half of its piers. By any grade school performance measurement, they failed;

➤ And a less than 1/5 chance that your fund would just be in the top 25% of funds.

Keep in mind, we are talking here ONLY about the best-of-the-best managers.

A second study by Vanguard ranging from 1990 to 2010 found the results may be even worse. Their study, which looked to find funds that consistently stayed in the top ranking, found that only 16% of funds remained in the top-tier after one year, 12% after 3 years, and 9% after 5 years[ii].

Didn't you hire a manager in the first place because they were better than average? Do you know if they still are? The chances aren't in your favor.

When you look further at the data in the following graph, one thing stands out. No matter what the type of stock, you have little chance to beat a simply Prudent Buying or Price-Taker strategy.

Another strategy advisors like to sell is look to the small cap and international small cap areas as having some potential for Gamblers to outperform.

On first look you may think that this may be true for the small international area of the market. As we will discuss later, this is just a flaw in the data. Living in our data on demand world, we sometimes do not realize the strides our databases and indices have made in only a years to remove concerns.

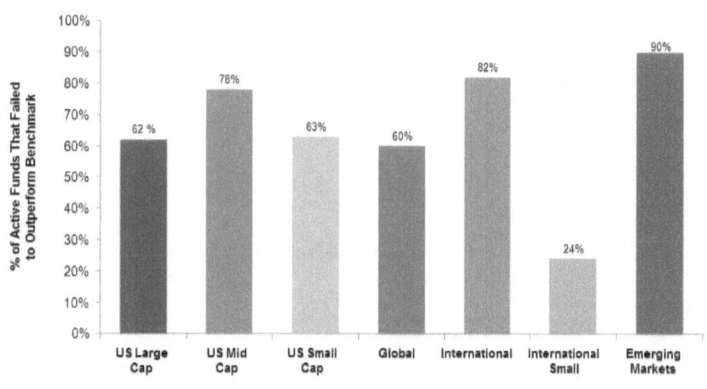

The Failure of Active Management
Percentage of Active Public Equity Funds That Failed to Beat the Index
Five Years as of December 2010

Source: Standard & Poor's Indices Versus Active Funds Scorecard, year end 2010. Index used for comparison: US Large Cap—S&P 500 Index; US Mid Cap—S&P MidCap 400 Index; US Small Cap—S&P SmallCap 600 Index; Global Funds—S&P Global 1200 Index; International—S&P 700 Index; International Small—S&P Developed ex. US SmallCap Index; Emerging Markets—S&P IFCI Composite. Data for the SPIVA study is from the CRSP Survivor-Bias-Free US Mutual Fund Database.

Case Study – Bill Miller

If you need even further proof that Gambling is a flawed investment strategy, let's consider the case of one of the most successful Gamblers in history, Bill Miller.

Miller of the Legg Mason Capital Management Value Trust (LMNVX) had a winning streak of beating the S&P 500 every calendar year for 15 consecutive years from 1991 through 2005.

Just after he achieved this feat, his performance suffered. From 2006 through 2010 Miller's fund placed in the bottom 5% of his peers in four out of five calendar years.

Legg Mason versus S&P 500 -- 2006 through 2010

Growth of Wealth
Monthly: 01/2006 - 12/2010; Default Currency: USD

See Standardized Performance Data & Disclosures.
Selection of funds, indices and time periods presented chosen by client's advisor. Indices are not available for direct investment and performance does not reflect expenses of an actual portfolio. Past performance is not a guarantee of future results. Graph represents a hypothetical investment of $1. Performance includes reinvestment of dividends and capital gains.
The S&P data are provided by Standard & Poor's Index Services Group.

	2006	2007	2008	2009	2010
% Legg Mason Cap Mgmt Value (LMNVX)	6.92	-5.73	-54.61	41.96	7.71
% Rank in Category	98	98	99	6	96

During the good years, Miller achieved his goals by taking outsized bets. During the bad years he refused to invest in certain high-growth areas of the market like energy, and took large gambles on financials and mortgage companies before the financial crash of 2007.

Investors who experienced the many good years with Miller had to decide, will he turn things around, or continue to struggle? Through the first six months of 2011 Miller's fund continues to underperform, and as of this writing is in the 94th percentile of large-cap managers.

Become the gambler

The problem with working with a Gambler isn't simply that you trust someone else to make large bets with your money. You also have to be a Gambler yourself.

Ask yourself, if this was a manager that you believed would deliver outsized returns, at what point would you know to fire them?

The bet with having a Gambler becomes two-fold; you have to trust them to win, but when they don't, you have to bet you will fire them at the right time.

There is a mutual fund company called the Masters' Select Funds. The Masters' funds only hire the best mutual fund managers available who also manage other funds, and allow them to manage a portion of their funds' investments. They hire the 'masters.' This fund company, which does nothing but analyze the best Gamblers that money can buy, and hire and fire them, had Bill Miller as one of their managers during this period. They did not fire Miller until late 2008, well into his decline and right before he actually had a rebound year.

It is worth considering, **if a fund that is an expert at hiring and firing the best Gamblers got their own timing completely wrong, what chance do you or your advisor have?**

Bond gamblers

How do the results turn out for bond mutual funds? Incredibly similar.

There are well known bond managers who take exceptional risk, and use products in their funds that do not meet the needs of Stability, so there is the chance that some bond fund managers outperform their respective indices.

As you can see from the following chart, there is some level of over performance in the top 50% (now, almost 50% of the top 25% funds from 2001 – 2005 maintain a ranking in the top 50% of funds from 2006 through 2010.

Interestingly, again almost 1/3 of funds disappeared.

Subsequent Performance of Top 25% of US Bond Funds
As of December 31, 2010

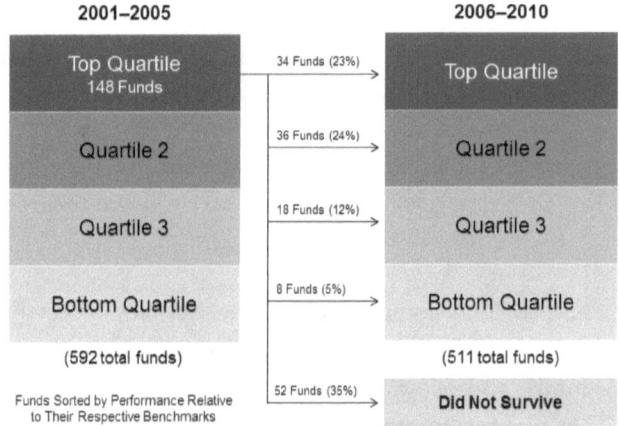

The left column represents all US bond funds in the CRSP Mutual Fund Database with a complete return history for 2001–2005. The funds are sorted by performance relative to their benchmarks. Funds in the top quartile are then tracked and directed to their subsequent performance quartiles in the following five-year period (2006–2010), or to the 'did not survive' category. Quartiles in the following period reflect all funds with a complete return history. Percentages may not total 100% due to rounding.

Data Source: CRSP Survivor-Bias-Free US Mutual Fund Database.

Conclusion

Hopefully I have put to rest Gambling as a valid investment strategy. The results are clear. For all of the time you can spend researching, monitoring, and worrying over the performance of your investment funds, the best you can hope for is a small chance your fund will perform decently, and as good of a chance your performance will be so bad that the fund disappears. Wouldn't your time and money be better spent elsewhere?

The question remains if active management doesn't add value; if successful managers can't be determined; if managers survive due to luck; if there is no value after mutual fund manager fees; if it adds risk; if it results in unintentional investing… *then why do the majority of advisors recommend Gamblers for portfolios?*

The answer is not as complex as you may believe. **Advisors couldn't provide a service at a price clients would willingly pay if they didn't have to lend their 'expertise' at picking Gamblers to your portfolio strategy.**

Further Information:

➤ Barras, Laurent, Scaillet, O. and Wermers, Russ R., **False Discoveries in Mutual Fund Performance: Measuring Luck in Estimated Alphas** (April 20, 2009). *Journal of Finance*, Forthcoming; Swiss Finance Institute Research Paper No. 08-18; Robert H. Smith School Research Paper No. RHS 06-043. Available at SSRN: http://ssrn.com/abstract=869748

Price-Taker (Indexing)

The next common approach to investing is that of a Price-Taker. The Price-Taker seeks to determine what the allocation will be, and once established to buy 'the market' in those areas. It is also commonly referred to as indexing, after the market indexes a portfolio will seek to mimic. It is one of the forms of investing known as 'passive investing' because it does not gamble, but owns everything.

As an investment strategy, Price-Taking isn't a horrible way to go. Price-Taking in fact forms the foundation of the investment philosophy we recommend. Though there are a few items to consider before implementing a purely Price-Taking philosophy.

Why Price-Taking

Why do I refer to indexing as Price-Taking?

Indexing is a sound investment strategy. But, as an investor we should not only be concerned about owning the right assets, but purchasing them at the best price. An index Price-Taking strategy is only concerned about owning the market; there is no further consideration towards the buying of the investments other than if it involves owning the market.

In investing, you make money by selling for a price above the price you purchase. So, there is a consideration aside from we own. We want to make sure we purchase and sell at the best possible price.

If the market changes, a Price-Taker must change their portfolio with it, no matter the cost. For example, when a new company capitalizes itself with a stock offering, in order to receive the market return, a Price-Taker must own that stock. And you have to own it now. Because of the urgency in purchasing, you are not a picky buyer. You just have to buy.

Index Re-alignment

Think if you owned a flower shop business that had to purchase its flowers for inventory on a daily basis. Imagine every day the price of the items you need could be different.

And, imagine as a busy professional you call in your order at the same time of day of the same day of the week.

What do you think happens if your supplier realized you placed your orders this way? Do you think they're willing to look for deals, discounts, cut your costs when they know they have a guaranteed buyer who calls day-in and day-out like clockwork? Do you believe they are worried you might shop around for your inventory?

Of course not! They may not lower prices until after they know your order has been called in and filled.

Taking this a step further, let's now say every year the neighboring town has an event on the same day that you place orders which drives prices up.

Do you robotically place your order at the same day / time knowing you will pay more; or do you strategically place your orders around this event?

This is probably not an analogy that fits most businesses, but it explains how Price-Takers purchase stocks. They have to buy stocks regularly; they can't plan around prices. They have to buy stocks when added to their particular index; they can't plan around days. They have one goal: to buy that stock. Not with consideration for price. Or fees. Or if the price is temporarily high due to speculation, odd events, or any other reason. Or if the company is a higher risk than we originally believed. An index may keep a bad investment (Enron) for much longer than we would prefer.

The chart below shows how speculation makes Price-Takers pay more for stocks. The price runs on the chance of an index result in Price-Takers paying 2-4% more for large stocks than what appears to be a normal value based on the preceding and following prices.

The Effect of Index Reconstitution on Stock Prices

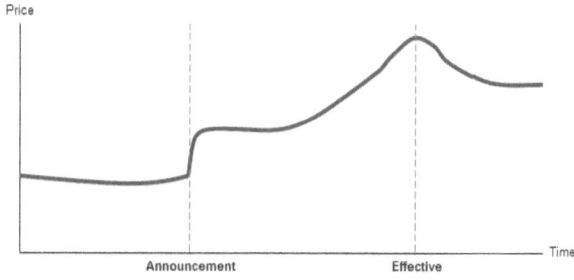

* Stocks rise on announcement of inclusion.
* Index funds are forced to buy high on effective date.
* Buying and selling to track index changes reduces tracking error but generates transaction costs.

	S&P 500 Index	MSCI EAFE Index
One-Day Return after Announcement (%)	3.2	3.4
Run-Up to Effective Date (%)	3.8	4.5
Decay after Effective Date (%)	-2.1	-2.6

S&P 500 data source: Anthony Lynch and Richard Mendenhall, "New Evidence on Stock Price Effects Associated with Changes in the S&P 500 Index," *Journal of Business* 70, no. 3 (July 1997): 351-83. MSCI EAFE Index data source: Rajesh Chakrabarti, Wei Huang, Narayanan Jayaraman, and Jinsoo Lee, "Price and Volume Effects of Changes in MSCI Indices: Nature and Causes," *Journal of Banking and Finance* 29, no. 5 (May 2005): 1237-64. For illustrative purposes only. Past performance is not a guarantee of future results.

On the chart below, look at the relative volatility of the lower line to the upper. The lower line represents how the index investors in the small company stock area may not receive a consistent allocation to their index. You can see that over time, if you had bought into an index, that you begin the year with a strong weighting to the bottom 10% small stocks of the market, but end the year with something that looks completely different.

Annual Index Reconstitution Effects
Consistency of Asset Class Exposure

Percentage of Assets in Bottom 10% of Market	Russell 2000 Index	CRSP 6-10 Index
June 30 Averages (reconstitution month)	96.46	96.08
May 31 Averages (11 months after reconstitution)	88.46	96.83

- Over time, securities within an index can migrate from one asset class to another (such as from small cap to large cap).

- An index's characteristics may be significantly different 11 months after reconstitution due to security migration.

- An index that purports to represent a certain asset class may not offer thorough, consistent exposure to the underlying risk factors.

The spikes in the bottom line tell us two things:

➤ After eleven months the fund does not look like the fund we purchased. We therefore hold an investment we did not intend to.

➤ A full year afterwards this fund has to sell certain stocks and buy others as a Price-Taker.

Imagine for a moment that you are a savvy speculator. If you know that a fund that has to follow the market will have to buy a significant amount of stocks (in this case small stocks) in order to meet its mandates, and that they are a Price-Taker – what would you likely put yourself in position to do? Sell them the stocks. And since they do not care what they price is, you buy them at today's price, knowing that you will have a buyer for them tomorrow at a higher price.

Variations of the Price-Taker strategy you will find from financial advisors are to only Price-Take certain areas of the market and Gamble others, or to take use Price-Taking investment vehicles like index funds and Gamble with them. Clearly since both involve Gambling, neither option is investing with intention. Advisors who use these approaches for the most part understand that there is value in a **pure** Price-Taking approach, but cannot admit that they themselves can add value to their clients' accounts without Gambling.

Be a Prudent Buyer

The third strategy and the one I've come to use for my clients is to what I call Prudent Buying. It is based on a owning the market, a dedication to lowering the costs to do so, and a scientific method for determining how to weight the stocks that are bought.

The chart below shows how Prudent Buying, or Asset Class Management, differs from Price-Taking and Gambling.

Value Added: Efficient Market Investing

Prudent Buying (Asset Class Management)
- Grounded in the efficiency of capital markets.
- Captures specific dimensions of risk identified by academic research.
- Minimizes transaction costs and enhances returns through trading and engineering.

Price-Taking (Index Management)	Gambling (Active Management)
•Accepts asset class returns.	•Attempts to beat the market through security selection and market timing.
• Allows commercial benchmarks to define strategy.	•Undermines asset class exposure to keep up with the most "promising" securities.
•Sacrifices transaction costs and turnover in favor of tracking.	•Generates higher fees, trading costs, and tax consequences due to increased turnover.

Prudent Buying Versus Gambling

Perhaps the best way to understand Prudent Buying is to compare how it is different from the other two strategies.

It is June 2011 and my alma matter, a consistently top tier NCAA football contender, has in the past month revealed several scandals; players and recruits have transferred to other schools; the coach did not reveal he was aware of the issues and later resigned; and we still do not know if there will be penalties including forfeiting post-season opportunities or scholarships.

Just six months ago the program competed in a BCS bowl game, and had arguably the best recruiting class in the conference. Sports analysts had placed them again in the top of their division and in the top 10 nationally.

Sports analysts, like stock analysts and other Gamblers, do not have more information than others do in order to avoid catastrophes like the scandal above. No one came out six months ago and said to avoid my alma matter next season because they were about to hit a rough patch. Just the same, they don't pick the winners consistently.

Prudent Buying is different from gambling in that it makes almost no attempt to time the market. It makes almost no stock picks because it owns almost everything. In football terms, Prudent Buying suggests it is better to bet on the sport of football and that college fans will still be filling the seats in all stadiums, than it is to bet on a team. Because no matter what you think about them today, their outlook could change completely tomorrow. It recognizes there will be winners, and losers, and attempts to capitalize on the combined positive movement of the sport.

Prudent Buying Versus Price-Taking

You may be part of the majority of Americans who buys gas for a car on a regular basis. If so, or if you have ever lived with someone who drives the following way you will be able to understand easily how Price-Taking varies from Prudent Buying.

I've known a lot of drivers who like to live on the 'E'dge – and by that I mean they keep the gas gauge just above 'E,' always putting a few dollars in to just make it to where they need to get.

Living that way makes you a Price-Taker for gas. Whenever you want to drive, you have to pay the going rate for gas. It doesn't matter if you pull over and the station wants $5, 8, or 10 per gallon. You might run out of gas, and you would have to pay any taxi or hitching costs to make it to a station, where you would again be a Price-Taker for the price of gas.

A Prudent Buyer drives the same route as a Price-Taker, but they have a strategy. Their tank is comfortably full, and only purchase gas on days they know prices are best, or on days they drive past a cheaper station. They make money by saving money by not having to pay the going price for gas on a given day, since they can always wait several days and monitor gas prices and their purchases.

As far as investing is concerned, in many ways a Price-Taker and Prudent Buyer have similar goals. A Price-Taker wants to own the market and achieve the markets return. A Prudent Buyer will also own the market, but they want to keep more of their money by not spending as much to own the market. A Prudent Buyer will also always buy gas for their car. They just buy it according to a plan.

And the plan changes! You might buy your gas on Tuesdays for the most part, finding that it is cheapest, but you may delay due to a holiday, or any number of reasons. Being a Prudent Buyer allows for flexibility in buying. But, just as your car will run out of gas if you do not refill, the flexibility is not all that great that you are Gambling on your purchases. In addition, there is a method to the relative asset allocation of stocks or bonds in the portfolio. The subject is far beyond the scope of this book, but for our purposes it is important to know that there is a method behind the process.

Prudent Buying does not try to find ways the market might be wrong. Instead, it considers the ways the investors are compensated for taking risk, and invest in those strategies, while avoiding those that do not work. In the next section we will cover how to implement a successful investment plan, before discussing ideas that throw many investors off the proven path.

Implementation Solutions

What follows is a summary of the best practices I have found in constructing a portfolio with your advisor.

Own the Market

Both Price-Takers and Prudent Buyers diversify across the market to reduce your risk. By far, the most value and time lost in investing is in the activity of trying to pick the specific areas of the market that 'may' perform better than others. Remember, the current price of an investment reflects what millions of market participants suggest it is worth based on assumptions of future profits to be earned from it. The spontaneous sum of the thoughts of those millions of buyers and sellers sets the current prices of securities. Paying one person for their best guess versus the rest of the world of participants is simply not a sound strategy.

That doesn't mean that your allocation shouldn't account for the relative risks and returns of different types of investments. As we saw earlier, small stocks generally are riskier, and they provide more return than the broad-based market. We should invest in many types of stocks, small companies, international companies, emerging markets stocks, to diversify, and add return to a portfolio.

Trying to choose when the market has 'mispriced' a stock is fruitless. For every person that thinks the stock is underpriced, there must be someone willing to sell it to them who thinks it is overpriced.

Diversify Globally

The market is (and has for a long time been) a global one. From our beginnings as a country, we traded with other nations who produced certain items relatively more efficiently than us. We in turn gave them cotton, textiles, and items that we produced comparatively better than they.

Today, emerging economies provide us with many of these goods. Meanwhile, we have moved forward to offer higher profit goods and services. By diversifying globally, we not only profit from established companies and industries, but emerging ones.

The U.S. makes up about 40% of the world's market capitalization. To profit from companies that do well across the world, but are located in a foreign land, we need to be owners of those companies where we politically can feel an investment is worth the risk. A good company is a good company wherever its headquarters are located.

World Market Capitalization
$35.6 Trillion as of December 31, 2010

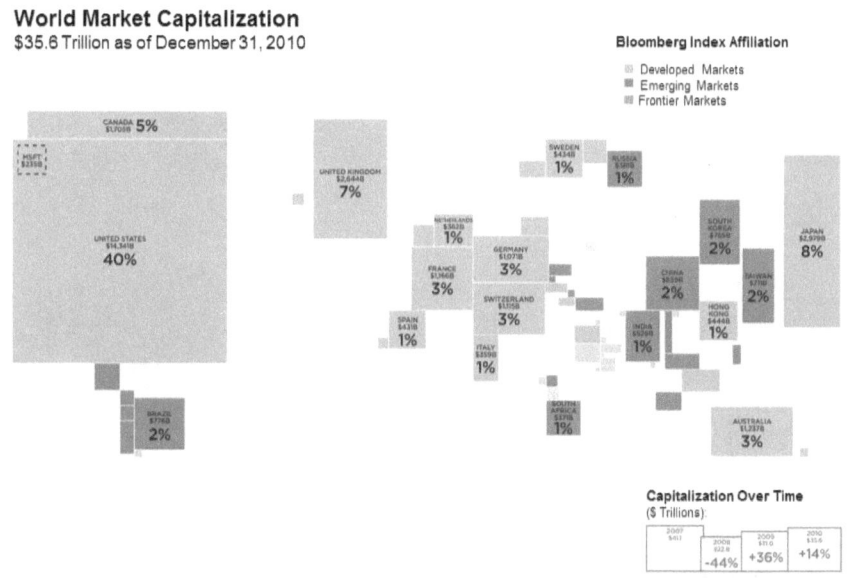

In US dollars. Market cap data is free-float adjusted from Bloomberg Securities Data. Many small nations not displayed. Totals may not equal 100% due to rounding. Dimensional makes case-by-case determinations about the suitability of investing in each emerging market, making considerations that include local market accessibility, government stability, and property rights, before making investments. For educational purposes; should not be used as investment advice. 1. An example large cap stock provided for comparison.

In undeveloped or emerging markets we should monitor the ability to be free owners of companies, own them where we can, and realize we are taking risks in the asset allocation decision. It has not been unheard of for communist countries to nationalize foreign assets. Many countries are just as well played in your portfolio by owning companies in developed countries who supply goods and services to the emerging economy.

Stay in the Market

The problem with trying to avoid the bad times is you often miss out on the good (and better) times. The chart below shows the consequence of missing the best and worst day, month, and months in the market. By attempting to avoid the worst periods, we most often miss out on the best periods, and only negatively impact our returns.

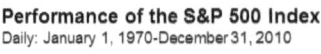

Performance of the S&P 500 Index
Daily: January 1, 1970-December 31, 2010

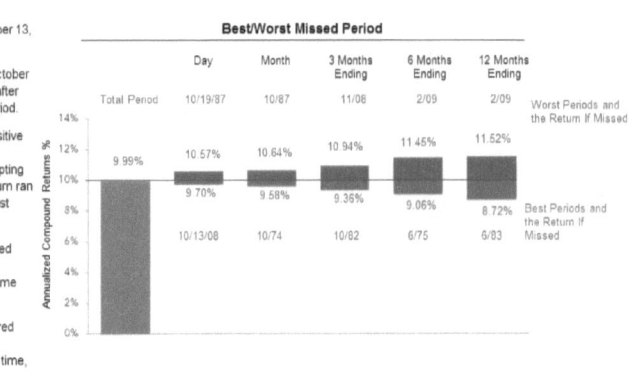

The best single day was October 13, 2008.

The best one-month return, October 1974, happened immediately after the second-worst one-year period.

The occurrence of strongly positive returns has been especially unpredictable. Investors attempting to wait out an apparent downturn ran a high risk of missing these best periods.

Nine of the top 25 days occurred between September 2008 and February 2009, during which time the S&P dropped 41.8%.

Five of the Top 10 days occurred between October 2008 and November 2008, during which time, the S&P 500 dropped 22.8%.

Time periods greater than one month are based on monthly rolling periods, and dates indicated are end of period.
The S&P data are provided by Standard & Poor's Index Services Group.
Indexes are not available for direct investment. Their performance does not reflect the expenses associated with the management of an actual portfolio. Dimensional Fund Advisors is an investment advisor registered with the Securities and Exchange Commission. Information contained herein is compiled from sources believed to be reliable and current, but accuracy should be placed in the context of underlying assumptions. This publication is distributed for educational purposes and should not be considered investment advice or an offer of any security for sale. Past performance is not a guarantee of future results. Unauthorized copying, reproducing, duplicating, or transmitting of this material is prohibited.
Date of first use: June 1, 2006.

During the market downturn in 2007-2008 I worked at a money management firm. I remember speaking with one client in particular who we had just invested his Rollover IRA into our growth strategy. We discussed his risk tolerance, and the client assured us he was investing for the long-term, and he insisted this was the strategy for him.

As it became clear the rough shape many of our financial institutions were in during 2008, and the market plunged, this client called in to discuss his concerns. He was convinced that the market was going to continue to drop for some time yet, and wanted to make sure he did what he could to preserve his wealth. He requested we move his account for cash for the time being.

We placed the order and moved to cash. The very next day Congress began to appear as though they would bailout the financial system. The markets were up 10% over the following days. Of course, I received a phone call from the client, who now felt good about the direction of things and wanted to go back into the markets. We discussed that just because it appeared things were better, that it didn't mean that the market may react how he would expect. We spoke about how investing was for the long-term, and in order to be successful he had to commit to a strategy. He was committed, he said, now that things were looking up.

No sooner than we invested did Congress get together and pass the bailout bill. And what was the result? The market dropped, and *dropped fast.*

Can you guess who called the next day? My client once again wanted to be out of the market.

What happened here? Due to investing based on emotions, thinking he knew what would happen, and trying to time the markets, this client: 1) sold at the market low, 2) permanently set his portfolio back 10% when the markets bounced back (we may not expect a 10% return over a year let alone several days), 3) bought back into the markets at a temporary high, 4) and finally, he wanted to sell (*again!*) after the market dropped, almost assuredly guaranteeing he would permanently miss out on the recovery.

Summing up the transactions, this investor probably put his portfolio back several years simply by gambling on the direction of the market in the short-run, and not believing in the long-run strategy.

Taking a look at the following graph, how can you possibly determine at pinpoint precision when the recovery will happen? The day after the market bottom of March 9, 2009 the Dow Jones was up 5.8%. The same response has occurred during many market declines; the recovery is as swift and unexpected as the downturn.

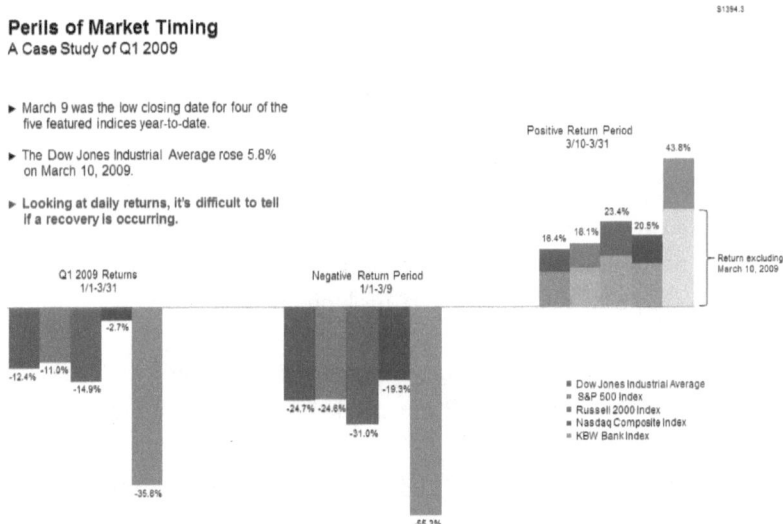

Perils of Market Timing
A Case Study of Q1 2009

S1394.3

► March 9 was the low closing date for four of the five featured indices year-to-date.

► The Dow Jones Industrial Average rose 5.8% on March 10, 2009.

► Looking at daily returns, it's difficult to tell if a recovery is occurring.

Returns are from market-close to market-close. Indices are not available for direct investment; their performance does not reflect the expenses associated with the management of an actual portfolio. The S&P data are provided by Standard & Poor's Index Services Group. Dow Jones data provided by Dow Jones Indexes. Russell data copyright © Russell Investment Group 1995-2010 all rights reserved. Mutual fund universe statistical data and non-Dimensional money managers' fund data provided by Morningstar, Inc. Nasdaq Composite Index data provided by The Nasdaq Stock Market, Inc. KBW Bank Index data provided by Keefe, Bruyette & Woods, Inc. (KBW). Past performance is not a guarantee of future results.

Increase Your Stability Overtime

Stability is the money we may use for expected future cash needs, and unexpected emergencies. As we age the amount we may use increases as our time horizon for using it decreases. So, increase your stability as you age.

Keep It Simple

Keeping things simple can be advantageous. The graph below shows how an extremely simple 60% Growth / 40% Stability portfolio performed against the professionally managed pension funds of the largest corporations.

Basic 60/40 Balanced Strategy vs. Company Plans
Results of 192 Corporate Pension Funds
Annual: 1988–2005

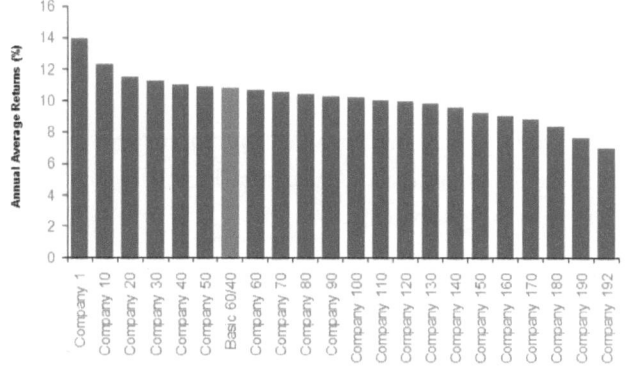

Companies
(in alphabetical order)

Anheuser-Busch Cos., Inc.
Avista Corp.
Cooper Industries, Inc.
Delta Air Lines, Inc.
Edison International
FirstEnergy Corp.
Goodyear Tire & Rubber Co.
Ingersoll-Rand Co. Ltd.
IBM Corporation
Jefferson-Pilot Corp.
Lincoln National Corp.
Sherwin-Williams Co.
Sunoco, Inc.
SunTrust Banks, Inc.
UAL Corp.
Union Pacific Corp.
Verizon Communications, Inc.
VF Corp.
West Pharmaceutical Svcs., Inc.
Williams Cos., Inc.
Wolverine World Wide, Inc.

Basic 60/40 is 60% S&P 500 Index, 40% Lehman Brothers US Government/Credit Bond Index Intermediate, rebalanced monthly.
Source: FutureMetrics (December 2006); all companies with fiscal year ending December, with complete return data from 1988-2005.
The S&P data are provided by Standard & Poor's Index Services Group. Barclays Capital data, formerly Lehman Brothers, provided by Barclays Bank PLC.

As you can see, this portfolio beat the managers of the majority of some of the largest pools of money there are. Add to it our portfolio isn't even all that diversified, simply being made up of the S&P 500 Index fund for Growth, and the Lehman Brothers (now Barclays) U.S. Government Credit Bond Index.

There is little potential upside to Gambling, and significant risk of underperforming and being unable to make up fees. With all of the resources and investment opportunities available to pension funds, the fact most cannot beat a very simple strategy is worth considering. You do not need complex financial products in your portfolio in order to achieve returns. In fact, the complex products available to pension plans are vastly superior to those available to the average multi-millionaire investor.

Keeping it simple in your mutual fund holdings also provides benefits. Continue reading the next section *Don't Play With Building Blocks* to see how costs begin to multiply by adding complexity to a Prudent Buyer portfolio.

Don't Play with Building Blocks

In an effort both to make things manageable, and to cut the costs you don't see, our Core Portfolio strategies at Clear Financial have been developed around a 'less is more' philosophy.

When we can, we recommend Growth funds that recognize that rebalancing costs time and money. Owning a portfolio full of mutual funds means that as stocks traverse the spectrum of stock classifications, a Price-Taking manager in one area of the market must be a buyer for that stock. Likewise, a manager in the classification that the stock moved away from must be a seller of that stock.

In an 'own the market' strategy, does it benefit us to own mutual funds who must sell stocks to other mutual funds we also own?

Our recommendations depend heavily on the client situation, but a Core Portfolio is simply the same portfolio of Growth stocks, owned in one or a few baskets instead of nearly a dozen or more. It removes walls between investment funds, creating a more cohesive portfolio, and limits the ability to invest with unintentional risk.

For example, you might own a U.S. portfolio, instead of a:

- ➤ Large Cap Growth fund
- ➤ Large Cap Value fund
- ➤ Mid Cap Growth fund
- ➤ Mid Cap Value fund
- ➤ Small Cap Growth fund
- ➤ Small Cap Value fund
- ➤ Micro Cap fund

And so on…

Many advisors recommend a building block approach to their portfolios. They pick an asset class – mid-cap value stocks for example – and then pick a fund or manager to fit into that asset class. They repeat this process of placing one or more funds into an asset class. What ends up occurring is the building block portfolio below.

A Traditional Portfolio of Mutual Funds
Advisors traditionally start with targets for each category of mutual fund, and then assign a fund manager to fill that need.

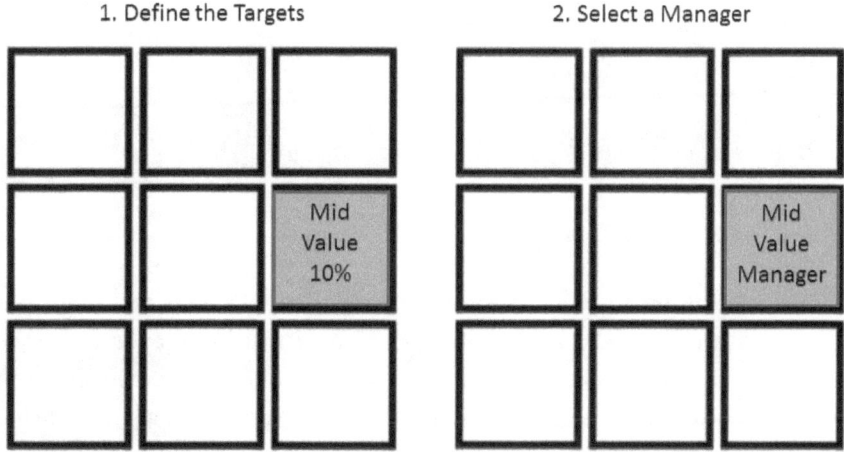

The Core approach gives us a solid foundation, and a complete portfolio, with less parts. By having between one and five funds, instead of a dozen or more, we incur significantly less costs as stocks move from one asset class to another. The beauty with a Core Portfolio is we follow the same approach to investing as we would have with a dozen or more funds.

Building Blocks can Increase Portfolio Costs

As their underlying stocks change categories, managers must buy and sell in order to continue to meet their benchmark. A more integrated solution is to hold fewer funds that hold the entire stock universe, as opposed to holding many funds.

A Traditional Portfolio Design | An Integrated Stock Portfolio

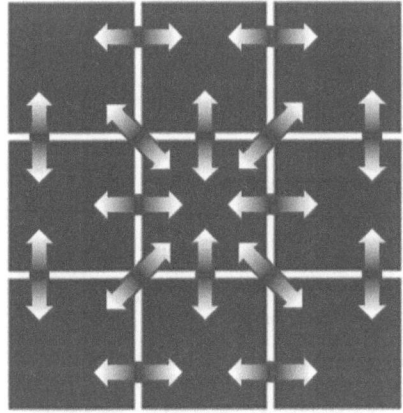 

The Core portfolio lets us cut costs in a few ways:

> **Transaction fees.** Rebalancing still occurs within the fund, but since it no longer includes sell a stock that has moved from one fund to another, the costs have decreased. A double-benefit is you also cut the fees associated with your personal rebalancing between funds.

> **You decrease your taxes.** As a fund sells a stock to buy it again in another fund, it causes a tax event.

The chart below demonstrates the amount of excess turnover in a building block approach for U.S. stocks alone can be over 30%.

Robert Schmansky, MA, CFP®

Traditional Asset Allocation Generates Excess Turnover

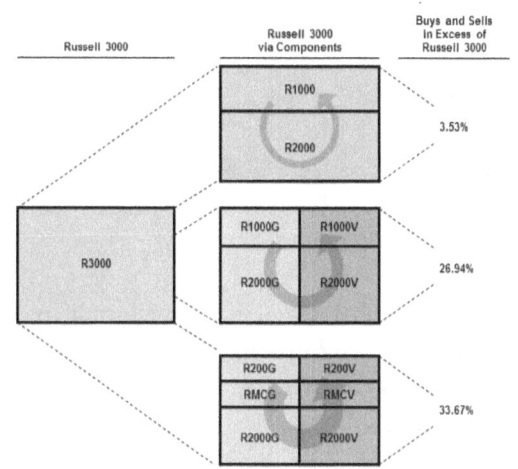

- In effect, a component portfolio buys and sells from itself, generating needless costs and taxable events.

Annual: January 1999–December 2010.
Russell components are Russell indices weighted according to Russell 3000 market value weights (buys and sells measured by the weight of each component).
Estimated annual cost assumes transaction costs of 50 bps. Russell data copyright ◆◆Russell Investment Group 1995-2011, all rights reserved.
For illustrative purposes only.

Where appropriate, we recommend some level of a Core portfolio, either on a global level, or at the U.S. / International / Emerging level.

Building blocks do have their uses, to either complement, or supplement a core portfolio. But there is more evidence that using them as a base is not effective, making portfolios more costly (and burdensome) than necessary.

Consider Going 65

Sometimes we like to drive fast, because it feels good to get to where we are going ahead of time. If you drive 85 you of course are taking a greater chance of getting a ticket, or worse. You lose control of your ability to avoid accidents ahead of you.

Likewise, if you load up on Growth, you may do better over time. You also may do much worse. The point here is that Growth is a risk over the short and mid-term. If you don't need to take a risk in order to meet your goals, don't.

Chances are very good you will get in trouble going faster than you need to. It's why our teachers always yelled at us about running in the halls, or the lifeguards about running on the pool deck. *The chances of stubbing your toe and hitting the deck increase the faster you go!*

In terms of your finances your toe stub may set you back enough to be concerned about your goals again. It may not be worthwhile to go fast just to go fast.

This is where financial planning comes into the picture. Do you know why you are taking risks to begin with? Does it get you closer to meeting your goals to take risks, or would you be more likely to achieve your goals by having more control over the car at a lower speed?

It is alright to take risks with money for long-term goals, or money that you don't need that perhaps you intend to go to heirs – they still may need to take risks, even with your anticipated gift.

If you don't need to take risks, why take the chance?

Account for Taxes

Since most advisors aren't experts at taxes, it is important to have at least one person on your professional team who is. I generally recommend two experts (not of the same firm) on your personal tax team:

➤ A CPA who prepares the return, is responsible for making sure filings and responses to tax inquiries are thorough and completed on time, and has an intricate knowledge of tax law and policy;

➤ An advisor who looks at the big picture, runs an analysis of tax strategies, and reviews the tax return and tax plan as a part of the overall strategy.

The CPA is generally more present and past oriented, while the advisor is generally more future oriented.

It is important that these individuals are not of the same firm, as mistakes can and do happen, and they are far more likely to be caught by people with different takes, processes, and procedures.

There are dozens of scenarios I've come across that have led me to believe that individuals should not simply rely on one advisor. While it may be convenient to work with an advisor who also prepares taxes, the most compelling reason to have two sets of eyes on the return is that *you* are responsible for the mistakes and penalties on your return. If your advisor intentionally or not is placing items on the return incorrectly, the penalties fall on *you*.

In the interest of brevity, I'll share just one example of why you want an advisor to understand, and be able to advise on your tax plan.

➤ **Retirement and missed opportunities.** Many clients I meet have a significant amount of money coming to them in the year of retirement. This may be from cashing out vacation, options, stock or equity ownership in a business, and so on.

What occurs is usually a year of very high income. Many times the year following retirement leads to low, or even negative, taxable income due to the state tax and other deductions paid in the year following retirement when the return is filed.

Negative taxable income is something that without proper planning, can lead to a significant missed opportunity. How significant? Well, you can basically make more income, and pay no taxes. Zero. Zip. None.

The planning implications here are huge. You could have taken advantage of tax-free income, perhaps by taking money from an IRA and converting it to a Roth where you have ensured all of the growth of that money too will never be taxed, had you properly planned.

If you insist on going to a stock-broker or insurance advisor as your primary financial advisor, realize you need to work with an incredible CPA who knows more about you than most tax preparing CPAs do to not miss opportunities like the above. Even the best CPAs may be more present oriented, and miss future planning opportunities like the above.

I find it is better to work with an advisor who can be that second set of eyes, and who can question the CPA on your behalf. That is also why I recommend your advisor not do your taxes. In addition to being extremely busy for 25-50% of the year on tax preparation issues, you lose the most 'in tune' person with your plan on your team during tax preparation time.

Make Inheritances a Part of Your Plan

Too often though I see people make two mistakes when it comes to their inheritances:

> ➤ *Having an emotional attachment to the funds, and not changing.* They are often not willing to make changes, either out of fear of losing money due to their changes.

> ➤ *Not incorporating into their plan.* The inherited pot becomes a separate pot. In some cases that is acceptable, for example in the case of a second marriage where the money should flow to the children of the inheriting spouse. But, even if it is in a separate account, it should be managed according to your needs.

The money or securities you received was a part of a plan – *someone else's* plan. And they wanted you to make it a part of your plan. That may involve shifting it between the *G / P / S* investments, but it is important to remember that money is simply a tool. Making it the most effective tool for you is what your loved one would have wanted.

Keep your Stability Funds Stable

As we've noted previously, it is important that your Stability funds actually be stable, or else they do not serve our purpose. There is little potential additional value in making them unstable, and so I want to hammer home the point here that it is a part of the plan to keep your Stability stable, no matter the yield.

> ➤ **Little reward for risk.** There has been almost no reward for risking your money into bonds of a moderate or lower quality. At the same time you add risk to your portfolio by doing so. If you are not compensated for the risk, then it is not a worthwhile investment.

> ➤ **Little reward for buying long-term bonds.** Likewise, there is almost no benefit to buying long-term bonds. The chart below shows that while increasing your maturity slowly increases your yield, the risk increases at a far more significant pace.

Evaluating the Maturity Risk/Return Tradeoff
Quarterly: 1964–2010

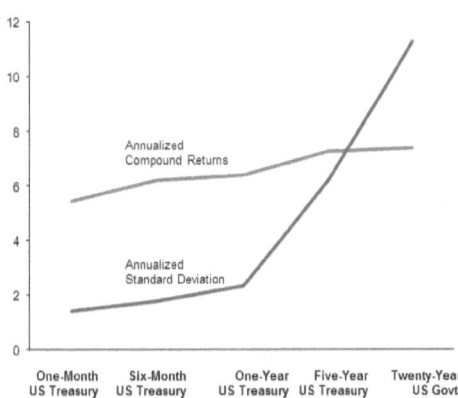

- Not all investors define risk as standard deviation. Some investors may seek to hedge long-term liabilities using long-term bonds.

- Historically, longer-maturity instruments have higher standard deviations than shorter-maturity instruments.

Maturity	One-Month US Treasury Bills	Six-Month US Treasury Bills	One-Year US Treasury Notes	Five-Year US Treasury Notes	Twenty-Year US Govt. Bonds
Annualized Compound Return (%)	5.45	6.20	6.41	7.27	7.37
Annualized Standard Deviation (%)	1.42	1.77	2.34	6.21	11.29

With bonds, the risk over the long-term is that the $1 you placed into the fund and expect to receive back, will not be worth $1 later. The longer you go, the more likely that is to being the case.

What we get with long-term and high-yield bonds are securities with risk characteristics often more closely aligned with Growth, and yet the returns are still in line with Stability. The risk of Growth and the returns of Stability make this a poor investing strategy since we aren't compensated for the risk we are taking.

Bond Funds Versus Individual Bonds

There is no fantastic reason to pick bonds over bond mutual funds, or vice versa. There are reasons to use one versus the other, but frankly there is not much downside to picking one over the other, despite what advocates of either approach claim. At Clear Financial Advisors we use both, depending on the appropriateness of the situation.

If you want to match a short to mid-term liability to a specific bond, buying a safe, individual bond can provide stability and comfort that this expense is covered in the portfolio. I wrote more about this topic in my booklet on the subject of bond ladders formed from individual bonds titled *Avoid Retirement Clumsiness*.

In general, the longer the time horizon, the more bond funds make sense. The global currency story is changing on an almost weekly basis, and there is a lot of reason for that to continue. Because of this, it makes sense to diversify your Stability holdings by use of a bond mutual fund. We recommend the Prudent Buyer approach as well in bond buying.

Buy Institutional, Not Retail

Retail mutual fund investing versus institutional investing is to the shopping world what a retail shopping experience is to having a private shopper. The experiences are completely different, and only one involves the store viewing you as an important client versus an ordinary customer.

Because their clients are generally smaller and 'unknown,' many retail fund families have been involved in scandals and practices that do not reflect the level of stewardship we recommend from the holder of your investment money. Certain funds have allowed privileged investors to gain illegally from the others, most market to other investors and advisors by spending your money to do so, and they generally are not concerned about keeping their internal costs low as they are about their level of profit.

Likewise, retail mutual funds (the ones that last) experience retail-like customers. What I mean by this is that they come and go, they are not loyal to the companies, and this add significant costs to the investors that stay. Think of a five-star restaurant versus a fast food experience. You would probably never see a middle school baseball team dining at the five-star restaurant since they don't generally cater to that customer. But, since the retail space does cater to these customers, you, as the next customer, pay the costs to live with the mess they leave behind.

When you work with institutional fund companies, as we do at Clear Financial, you do not have the retail investor experience. Not all institutional class funds are run the same, but in general the funds know more about their customers (the advisors and institutions that recommend them to clients), and many do attempt to be better stewards of their clients' money.

Don't Get Hung Up on Others Performance

The first rule of performance is… *don't believe the talk about performance.*

Don't believe what you hear about performance. When discussing performance with your friend, uncle, relative, neighbor, co-worker, boyfriend, girlfriend, spouse… it is critical to realize what you are hearing is:

1) not audited,

2) not likely that the facts have been completely unmolested,

3) not compared to a meaningful benchmark,

4) likely to be luck *if* real,

5) based on their financial plan (assuming there is one), risk tolerance, and goals, and not yours.

The second rule of performance is that ratings of professional performance is backward looking, and like any method of measurement, can be manipulated. Ratings are important to fund inflows (which impact manager bonuses), so managers do attempt to position their portfolios in order to look more attractive in their categories from a rating perspective.

Here are just a few methods that managers use to make sure get good ratings:

> *By not investing in the assets you hired them to.* This is what I've referred to as 'burying risk' within the portfolio or unintentional investing. By investing with riskier assets, they know they will in general earn a higher return than their peers by risking your money, and making your plan an unintentional one.

> *Closing poor performing funds.* Fund companies often have several funds open in the same investment category, and if one encounters a bad period they tend to fold losers into the winners. This reoccurring removal of losers makes their current group of funds appear as though they have more winners... but simply showing the investor the performance of an investment they didn't own doesn't recoup the money lost in a losing investment.

> *Luck.* Many recent studies have shown the vast majority of successful investors have simply been lucky. And by vast majority I mean almost all.

Fund Ratings

Everyone can relate to the desire to invest with highly rated managers. But, you probably can also relate to 'gaming' a system you know the mechanics of in order to appear to be doing better than you may otherwise.

Whenever there are numbers to meet, there are ways of manipulating those numbers to meet goals, and in investing it comes at the expense of an investor. If you are a fund manager and lose, it's alright; all you have to do is transfer the loser fund assets into winning fund, or hit the reset button and start a new one. Hey, it's not your money, why worry about losing it?

In judging a fund based on ratings, you also have a problem of deciding which rating service to believe. Morningstar is a popular service, but there are other qualified outlets that rate funds. Looking below at the chart of four funds, it is easy to see how one might not know who to trust will pick the most winning fund managers.

The Limits of Fund Rating Services

	Fund A	Fund B	Fund C	Fund D
Morningstar (Dec 2000)	★★★★★	★★	★★★	★★★★
Forbes (Dec 2000)	C	A	A+	D
US News & World Report (Dec 2000)	34	50	10	93
Wall Street Journal (Jan 2001)	E	C	A	B
BusinessWeek (Jan 2001)	A	No Rating	B+	C

Funds A, B, C, and D are actual funds. They are not identified because the purpose of this illustration is to emphasize that ratings, by themselves, do not provide enough information to make a sound investment decision.

Morningstar: Five stars is highest rating; one star is lowest rating.
US News & World Report: 100 is highest rating; 1 is lowest rating.

Since we can't tell from a rating if a fund is a good investment, and since a funds rating is based on past performance, is there a way we can use ratings to determine if a fund is a good investment for the future?

Yes. A better predictor of which funds may do best may just be a funds fees. Since fees are a hurdle that managers need to overcome, it has been shown that the lower the fees, the better chance of outperformance.

The above isn't to say that ratings can't be a part of a decision, but they certainly should not be the only part, and certainly is not the most important. Of greater importance is whether or not a fund fits within the portfolio needs.

There are newer rating categories I do recommend reviewing in combination with those that simply measure performance. These ratings, often called stewardship ratings, measure non-performance items such as:

➤ How much money managers have in their own investments,

➤ Investor stewardship history, and

➤ Record of regulatory complaints and issues.

While there are only a few ratings services who go into this depth of detail, often the best method is just to do your own internet search of an investment manager with keywords to search out regulatory problems.

Don't Get Hung-up On Your Performance

If you take all of the advice in this book and invest as a Price-Taker or Prudent Buyer, you really have no need to spend much time at all watching the market.

Why? Because we have a plan to capitalize on the characteristics of the markets that benefit us through *G / P / S Investing*™. We are not gambling based on what happened yesterday, and we have assets in our portfolio that people will find desirable to purchase in the future.

As a Price-Taker, you believe in the market price, and so whatever the market price is, that is exactly what it should be.

As a Prudent Buyer, you are allowing a manager to take advantage of others needs to buy at any price in the moment to make additional gains.

Because of this, your performance in either case will be related to the risk you take in the portfolio construction.

Trading on ratings

When you concern yourself with short-term performance, say when the star rating of a mutual fund declines, this is generally after a period that the manager did poorly. You may be selling at a low-point for that particular investment, only before it begins to increase as its strategy comes back into favor.

Likewise, if you sold a fund at its low, you are likely considering moving into a higher rated fund that has done exceptionally well recently. You may be buying into this fund near the peak of its strategy, only to find the manager underperforms going forward.

Here is what I see time and time again from investors who gamble, or who work with advisors who gamble on their behalf:

| Fund | Performance (Rank in Category) | | | | | Thru |
	2006	2007	2008	2009	2010	6/22/2011
CGM Focus Fund (CGMFX)	14.92% (41)	79.97% (1)	-48.18% (96)	10.42 (99)	16.94 (35)	-7.61 (100)
Fairholme Fund (FAIRX)	16.72% (23)	12.35% (10)	-29.70% (6)	39.01% (9)	25.47% (1)	-7.76% (99)

Many investors and advisors were lured into the high flying performance of the CGM Focus Fund (CGMFX) in 2007 after it returned nearly 80% for the calendar year, placing it in the top spot for large funds by a long shot.

Note that I did say above that many investors and advisors were lured into CGM *after* 2007.

Moving forward to 2008 we saw a reverse in fortune for the fund, when it lost nearly half its value, placing it in the bottom 5% of funds. Brought in by the high flying returns, investors would have lost half of the value of their investment in 2008. Even if they had invested for all of 2007, the year its returns blew most funds out of the water, those investors were still negative from 2008 and 2009.

Granted, 2008 was an anomaly in the markets, and so one might suspect the CGM fund simply had an off year. Even though we are paying for a manager to do better, it isn't possible for their strategy to work every year.

In 2009 the market recovered and we saw most funds that lagged in 2008, outperform in 2009 (note: this might be an indication that your manager simply takes more risk than you intend if they perform better in up markets and worse in down). But, not the CGM fund. While it was up 10.42% for the year, it is important when using a Gambler to compare them in terms of their peers. Earning 10.42% in 2009 was actually a dismal return for Growth for the year, and the fund performed even worse on a relative basis, placing in the 99th percentile of large company funds.

And now the question to investors became – do I sell now, or wait for a recovery?

An alternative fund that many fled to had a similar story to CGM in 2007. Fairholme Fund (FAIRX) had placed in the 10% of funds in its category from 2007 through 2010. As investors fled to Fairholme, had they done so at the beginning of 2010 they would have had above par performance for the year. However, in the first half of 2011 Fairholme today is almost neck and neck with CGM, both funds scoring 99th and 100th in their categories respectively.

Research by Vanguard[iii] has confirmed that selecting funds based on star rating is a poor predictor of future performers. On average, the dismal 1-star funds were more likely (46% probability of positive excess returns) than the 5-star top performers (39%) to provide the excess returns you paid them for.

The golden rule of investing is to buy low, sell high. The strategy of flipping out of funds regularly based on ratings promotes the opposite: buy high, sell low. Investors grabbed these funds generally after high years when the managers luck was good, rode them down, and repeated the process of buying high, selling low with a new manager.

The beauty of investing as a Price-Taker or Prudent Buyer is that we don't have a manager taking outsized bets that place us at the extremes. Just the same, realizing that an allocation to the entire market on the whole will beat the majority of managers over time lets us know that we don't have to watch performance on a daily basis to know our Growth is performing exactly as it should, and better than most other alternatives.

In the *G / P / S Investing*™ system, when stocks decline in value, you have your Preservation and Stability that will often act as counterweights, lessening overall losses. This of course assumes you did not risk your Stability by reaching for a little more yield, because if you did you are more likely to lose it along with the losses in Growth (you can see how these strategies are interconnected… if that isn't intentional I don't know what is!).

Saboteurs and Myths of Intentional Investing

Whatever our approach, there are those that want to lure us away from investing, and towards gambling our hard earned wealth in the latest gimmick product or strategy. Whether it is an advisor with a product that does not fit into principles or a *G / P / S* strategy, or an publisher who wants to sell you a magazine, these are the common ideas that many fall victim to when attempting to be intentional with their investing.

Wait for Normal Times

Investors sometimes want to just wait for things to normalize before investing. It is exactly the wrong thing to do.

This attitude generally implies a link between the economy and the stock market. While it makes sense intuitively to believe one exists, let me assure you that if there is, it is that the market does not move in sync with the economy. The market is considered to be a *leading indicator* of the economy since it turns well before the economy returns to normal times.

The market price today is based on what the information about the future performance of the market will be. Generally, in bad times it means that we already have factored in plenty of bad times to continue. While people continue to look at bad signals as proof the market will continue to do poorly, the market considers the degree to which signals are not as bad as it may have priced into current stocks, and therefore it is generally found that the market is up well before the economy.

The chart below shows how the most risk in the market (the risk premium is the lowest) occurs at the time when businesses are operating at their highest in the business cycle. Meanwhile, when things are looking bad in the market, there is relatively less risk to investing.

Market Risk Premium Is Countercyclical

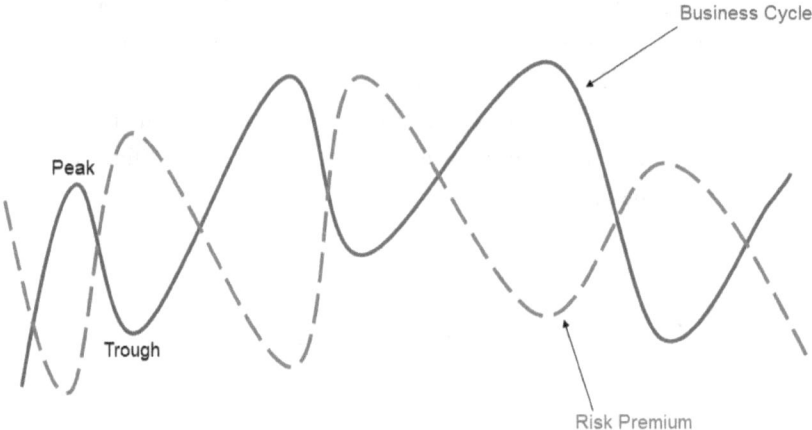

Business Cycle

Peak

Trough

Risk Premium

The risk premium is the additional return an investor requires to compensate for the risk borne. Business cycle is a repetitive cycles of economic expansion and contractions. Peak is the high point at the end of an economic expansion until the start of a contraction. Trough is the transition point between economic recession and recovery.

What is normal? If a diversified portfolio (60% Growth and 40% Stability portfolio) has a started deviation of 11.26%, that means a *normal* return will be between roughly 0% and 23%. Call me crazy, but I don't think most people find that 0% or 23% is normal. And add to that the fact that one out of every three years it will be better or worse.

And what about abnormal times? Shouldn't we wait for a 'return to normalcy' before trusting the investing climate?

The answer is no. The chart below shows the last several crashes which we have 5 year performance data following. Even after losing 17% during the one year following the 1973 OPEC Oil Crisis, the next two years brought the average annual return to 7%, and to 11% over the following four years. We see similar numbers for most time periods after declines. Being out of the market during the downturn and the time following is not the answer.

The Market's Response to Crisis
Performance of a Normal Balanced Strategy: 60% Stocks, 40% Bonds

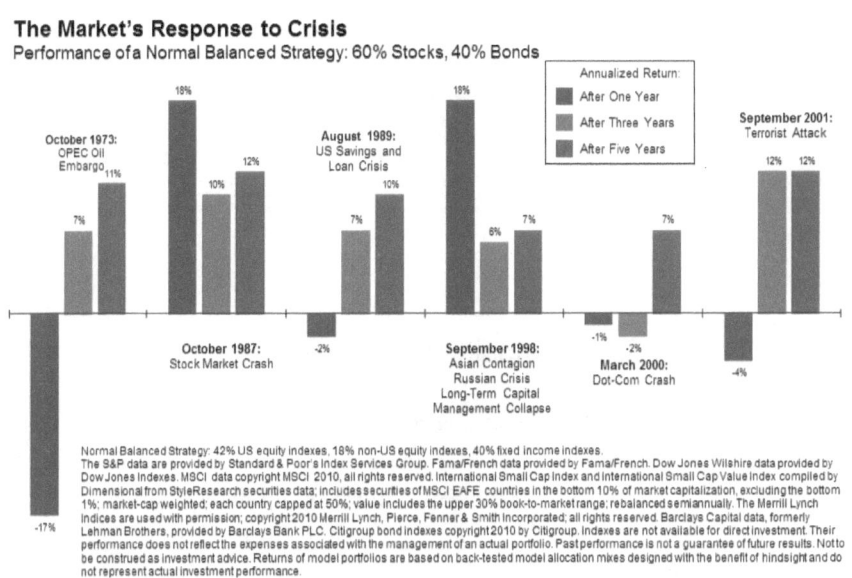

Normal Balanced Strategy: 42% US equity indexes, 18% non-US equity indexes, 40% fixed income indexes.
The S&P data are provided by Standard & Poor's Index Services Group. Fama/French data provided by Fama/French. Dow Jones Wilshire data provided by Dow Jones Indexes. MSCI data copyright MSCI 2010, all rights reserved. International Small Cap Index and International Small Cap Value Index compiled by Dimensional from StyleResearch securities data; includes securities of MSCI EAFE countries in the bottom 10% of market capitalization, excluding the bottom 1%; market-cap weighted; each country capped at 50%; value includes the upper 30% book-to-market range; rebalanced semiannually. The Merrill Lynch Indices are used with permission; copyright 2010 Merrill Lynch, Pierce, Fenner & Smith Incorporated; all rights reserved. Barclays Capital data, formerly Lehman Brothers, provided by Barclays Bank PLC. Citigroup bond indexes copyright 2010 by Citigroup. Indexes are not available for direct investment. Their performance does not reflect the expenses associated with the management of an actual portfolio. Past performance is not a guarantee of future results. Not to be construed as investment advice. Returns of model portfolios are based on back-tested model allocation mixes designed with the benefit of hindsight and do not represent actual investment performance.

Looking at it another way, when is the appropriate time to purchase? The stock market turns ahead of the economy, and so waiting for good economic news is a fruitless endeavor.

The following graph shows the last recession in the U.S. and the performance of the S&P 500. If you had waited for 'better times,' don't believe you would have invested at the end of the recession periods; most who subscribe to this philosophy wait a year or longer to invest in the markets again after the economy turns.

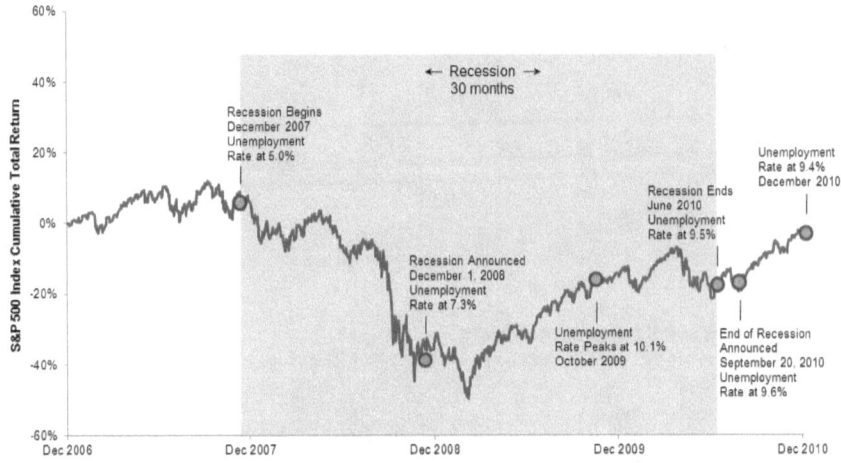

Recessionary Period
January 2007-December 2010

For illustrative purposes only.
Indices are not available for direct investment; their performance does not reflect the expenses associated with the management of an actual portfolio. Past performance is not a guarantee of future results and there is always the risk that an investor will lose money. Source: National Bureau of Economic Research (NBER) for economic expansions and recessions data; the S&P data are provided by Standard & Poor's Index Services Group; US Bureau of Labor Statistics for unemployment data.

Saving and Stability is not Safety

Saving is not enough when it comes to a long-term investment plan. Neither is having only a portfolio of Stability. While your principal may be safe, the amount that it can purchase may not keep up with inflation.

Fixed Annuities for Stability

Certain types of annuities can be appropriate tools to use as a part of a portfolio. Other annuities known as variable annuities and equity index annuities we will discuss later as products to avoid.

As too much of anything can be dangerous, so is too much Stability. Insurers, bank representatives, and insurance agents try to push *dollar stability* as *safety*, and ignore that inflation erodes Stability over time. There are risks we can see, and risks that only become evident over time. And while there are ways to deal with the inflation risk, it is not with a 100% Stability portfolio.

If you only invest a small portion of your money, it can make a significant difference. The graph below also shows us how holding a small portion of other investments can reduce the risks we face.

A 100% Stability Portfolio May Not Be Safest

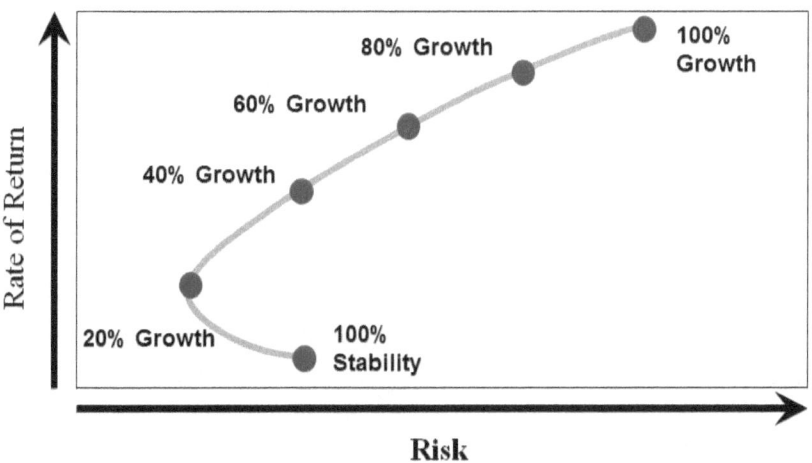

Having a little Growth provides diversification from the threats we face to our cash flow. It can be difficult to realize that there will be some fluctuation by adding growth, but we can't escape volatility in the world. Prices will fluctuation, and so the value in terms of purchasing power of your 100% stable portfolio will decrease.

Buying Bonds Based on Yield

Most often, the first question an investor asks when presented with a bond is – what is the yield?

When investing for stability, the important question however is – what are the chances we will lose our principal to default?

Investment yield is a function of how safe a bond is. If there is a higher risk that you will lose your principal, you will have a higher yield than comparable term bonds.

You can probably guess that risking your principal does not meet our purpose of stability, and so we do not recommend chasing yield on bonds, savings, or other stable accounts.

The better approach is to stay very safe with your Stability, and take risks with Growth where that risk is rewarded. The chart below shows the returns and volatility (standard deviation) of 5 portfolios. Portfolio 1 involves a simple Price-Taker portfolio of 60% stocks (made up of the S&P 500 index), and 40% in a fairly conservative bond index.

Portfolio 2 involves switching our bonds for very short-term, safe bonds. This lowers the volatility of the portfolio. Portfolio 3, 4, and 5 show a progression of diversifying into an increasingly diverse stock portfolio.

The end result is a portfolio that is almost identical in terms of volatility, but earned over 2% more per year from 1973 through 2010.

A Fully Diversified Portfolio
Quarterly: 1973–2010
Model Portfolio 5

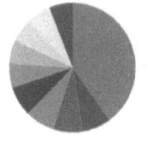

	Annualized Compound Return	Annualized Standard Deviation
Model Portfolio 1	9.47%	11.16%
Model Portfolio 2	8.83%	10.23%
Model Portfolio 3	9.74%	11.88%
Model Portfolio 4	10.68%	11.81%
Model Portfolio 5	11.65%	11.26%

- ■ Merrill Lynch One-Year US Treasury Note Index
- ■ S&P 500 Index
- ■ US Small Cap Index
- ■ US Large Value Index
- ■ Targeted Value Index
- ■ International Large Index
- ■ International Small Index
- International Large Value Index
- International Small Value Index
- ■ Emerging Markets Blended Index

	Barclays US Govt./Credit Bond Index	S&P 500 Index	BofA Merrill Lynch One-Year US Treasury Note Index	US Small Cap Index	US Large Value Index	Targeted Value Index	Intl. Large Index	Intl. Small Index	Intl. Large Value Index	Intl. Small Value Index	Emerging Markets Blended Index
Model Portfolio 1	40%	60%									
Model Portfolio 2		60%	40%								
Model Portfolio 3		30%	40%	30%							
Model Portfolio 4		15%	40%	15%	15%	15%					
Model Portfolio 5		7.5%	40%	7.5%	7.5%	7.5%	6%	6%	6%	6%	6%

Rebalanced annually. Barclays Capital data, formerly Lehman Brothers, provided by Barclays Bank PLC. The S&P data are provided by Standard & Poor's Index Services Group. The Merrill Lynch Indices are used with permission; copyright 2011 Merrill Lynch, Pierce, Fenner & Smith Incorporated; all rights reserved. Dimensional Index data compiled by Dimensional. Emerging Markets Blended Index consists of 50% Fama/French Emerging Markets Index, 25% Fama/French Emerging Markets Small Cap Index, and 25% Fama/French Emerging Markets Value Index. Fama/French Emerging Markets, Fama/French Emerging Markets Value and Fama/French Emerging Markets Small Cap Index weightings allocated evenly between Dimensional International Small Cap Index and Fama/French International Value Index prior to January 1989 data inception. Dimensional International Small Cap Value Index weighting allocated to International Small Cap Index prior to July 1981 data inception. International Value weighting allocated evenly between International Small Cap and MSCI World ex USA Index prior to January 1975 data inception. Indexes are not available for direct investment. Their performance does not reflect the expenses associated with the management of an actual portfolio. Past performance is not a guarantee of future results. Not to be construed as investment advice. Returns of model portfolios are based on back-tested model allocation mixes designed with the benefit of hindsight and do not represent actual investment performance. See cover page for additional information.

The takeaway here is simple. Diversify, take risks with Growth, and don't worry about the yield of your Stability. Worry about the safety of your Stability.

Buying Bond Funds Based on Past Performance

Chasing performance will also get you burned when buying bonds, for similar reasons to worrying about the yield.

To understand why, you need to understand why a fixed income manager is getting higher returns. In general, the only way to be paid more than the index is to risk your money, or gamble with options and derivative strategies. Since we are seeking stability, neither one of these options is attractive, as they both put Stability at risk.

To solidify the rebuttal against reaching for yield, let me share just two of several recent bond fund implosions, caused when managers of popular funds sought to earn just a little bit more than the market:

Schwab YieldPlus (SWYSX). Schwab YieldPlus is an ultra-short bond fund that was often used by advisors to provide a little more yield for cash accounts. Ultra-short term bonds are bonds that mature soon, and so we should expect that if we place our principal into the fund, that we will receive it back shortly, with interest.

As I write this in July 2011, I happen to have received several requests from the financial press to discuss how ultra-short bond funds and other investments can add a yield to your Stability investments. By the look of the graph of the Schwab YieldPlus fund below, does it appear as though it was worth it?

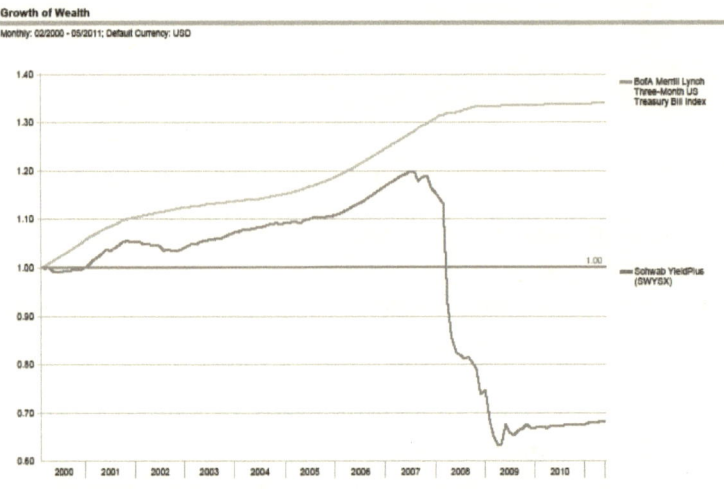

Growth of Wealth
Monthly: 02/2000 - 05/2011; Default Currency: USD

BofA Merrill Lynch Three-Month US Treasury Bill Index

Schwab YieldPlus (SWYSX)

See Standardized Performance Data & Disclosures.
Selection of funds, indices and time periods presented chosen by client's advisor. Indices are not available for direct investment and performance does not reflect expenses of an actual portfolio. Past performance is not a guarantee of future results. Graph represents a hypothetical investment of $1. Performance includes reinvestment of dividends and capital gains.
The Merrill Lynch Indices are used with permission, copyright 2010 Merrill Lynch, Pierce, Fenner & Smith Incorporated, all rights reserved.

While the desire to 'reach' for just a little higher yield is common, we need to simply look at history to realize the costs are much too great. By risking our Stability we not only put our safe money at risk, we eliminate the ability of a diverse portfolio to react to economic climates that might benefit true Stability.

The Reserve. The Reserve money market mutual fund holds two distinctions for being 'the first.'

➤ It was the first money market mutual fund.

➤ It was also the first to 'break the buck,' also known as losing money in money market terms.

Money market mutual funds target maintaining their value at $1.00. They have a mandate to maintain that $1.00 per share with short-term investments (in other words, it is meant to be absolutely stable). The Reserve fund was the first to close at a price other than $1.00, or "break the buck."

Prior to its collapse, The Reserve was paying a marginally higher yield than most other money funds. With prospective clients who were coming to us from brokerages, I noticed many not using the ordinary money market funds, but rather the company brokers had invested clients in The Reserve. This was likely to manage more of their money rather than simply recommending a safe, FDIC-insured bank savings or money market account.

When The Reserve broke the buck, it went through a lengthy liquidation process where investors were not able to access their money. Not only was this Stability investment not stable, it also was not available for use, defeating yet another purpose of Stability.

Reaching for just a little more yield is simply not a good investment strategy with Stability.

That being said, there are two ways that I agree with seeking higher performance than the market:

1) *Monitoring your bonds* to make sure they do not develop a risk of default, and selling bonds where risk develops. This involves watching the market on a frequent basis, as the bond market is often one of the best predictors of ill fortunes. I recommend doing this again through a Prudent Buying approach as opposed to Gambling since all of the reasons not to gamble in stocks apply to bonds as well, but also most bond Gamblers simply add risk to what we want to be Stability money.

2) A manager can buy *as a Prudent Buyer* in the bond market. In the case of bonds she will look at all of the bonds available at given time period, review where those bonds have been trading recently, analyze the reasons for any changes in price, and if the price is right, she may purchase that bond at a lower price than others.

In acting as a Prudent Buyer, they are still buying the same quality of bond, but simply at a point in time that offers an opportunity for profit.

Investing in High-Yield Bonds

High-yield, or junk, bonds, are more correlated to Growth than bonds. That means they put your Stability at risk by actually acting like Growth. By investing your Stability in higher risk, you just doubling down on risk, and not protecting yourself from deflation and stock market risk.

We only need to look to our principles to realize that markets work, and that in order to achieve a higher return, you must take more risk. Applied to Stability, we need to realize that the Stability markets work, and the yield you receive is related to the risk you take with your investment principal. But with Stability we know the risks are not worth the costs, and so don't fall victim to strategies promising a higher 'yield' or more 'income' with Stability. It's simply not worth the price you may pay.

This Time It Is Different

This is a common feeling about the current economic climate that leads many investors off the path of investing 'on purpose,' to being taken in an investing gimmick or unsound strategy.

Times are always different. We can agree on that point. And that is the place where any sales pitch for an improper investment idea comes into play.

It isn't what is different that is important in investing, but rather we need to pay attention to what is the same. Investing principles are the same. They are unchanging. Sadly though, so is the desire by many to convince you that they are different.

As long as people are allowed to transact freely, Growth will still seek to provide the highest returns, Preservation will protect against dollar inflation, and Stability will be a buffer against deflation.

The only concerns I have with *it* being different is that legislation will hamper one of the areas. And if it does, just like if you were to fill a surgeons rubber glove with water, when one of the fingers is pinched, the others will swell. Some area will do well, however just like guessing which finger in the glove will swell, it is nearly impossible to guess which sector will benefit consistently. When legislation restricts one area of investing, the money will flow from it and to the others.

By the way, government is one of the biggest interferences our market reacts to. And while Wall Street may be clever in allowing you to convince yourself of your need for their products because 'this time it is different,' I haven't seen a product yet that protects you from central bank induced inflation, taxes and tariffs on Growth, and their fear of fleeing Stability for various Preservation assets. I don't know a Gambler who can predict when news of legislation will come.

Your Workplace Plan May Not Be the Best Place to Save

Some financial advisors recommend saving more to your workplace plan, until you reach the maximum limits. While it *might* be true that this is your best option, that isn't always the case. In fact, if you are like many Americans, your workplace plan can be a simple way to save, but a poor place to invest. Workplace retirement plans often have high fees (including high hidden accounting fees), low diversification opportunities, and a lack of control that can make *simple* investing become *costly* investing.

A workplace plan can change at any time. You just don't know what will happen with your plan in the future, and yet in most plans your money is stuck, whatever those changes your employer decides for you may be.

Contribute up to the Maximum Match

Remember the chart we showed earlier of investment fees (page 8)? Many workplace plans have significant fees in the range of 2% or above. We already know the costs over time can reduce your portfolio by thousands and even millions of dollars.

Yes, the match is significant. Yes, all other things being equal you, it makes sense to take the free money that your employer offers. But, to ignore the impact of fees and a lack of diversification doesn't make sense. Most plans will have acceptable (though not ideal) costs and options, but after contributing up to the maximum match, don't take it as a given that your workplace plan is the best place to save.

Government Workers (Though Perhaps Everyone Soon)

Some workplace plans, such as the Thrift Savings Plan (TSP) for federal employees, require workers to turn their plan balance into an annuity in order to have health insurance benefits.

Keep in mind that an annuity is an investment for stability. An employee that would like to do the prudent thing, and roll their plan over to an IRA at retirement to invest it in a balance with growth and preservation, has no choice to do so if they would keep their medical benefits.

I suspect this will be a topic that we hear more about in the future, as the insurance industry has been pushing for more annuity plans for employees, and the government to this point has been appeasing them in congressional rulemaking committees. For now it is enough to realize how much lack of control in government sponsored retirement accounts is a reality.

Review Options for Moving Money Out

You may also want to review plan options for taking 'in-service, non-hardship' withdrawals. If your plan allows it, you may be able to roll part of your money while still employed over directly to an IRA account. If you are over 59½ you may have other options as well to explore.

There are plenty of issues with moving money from one account to another to know about before moving money from a 401(k), not the least of which is to have a plan in place to re-invest that money before doing so.

If you do move your money, it should be done directly to the new account custodian as a direct trustee-to-trustee transfer, and not as a 'rollover.' This means that the check is issued to the new IRA company, even if mailed to you. By going this route you avoid having a mandatory 20% withheld for taxes, which, if you do not want to pay tax on the money that was withheld for taxes, you have to come up with out of your own pocket within 60 days to put into the IRA.

Newsletter Services

Newsletters and online stock and fund selection websites are not held to high standards of performance reporting, and are not audited. There are a number of reasons why an investor would not, and some say cannot, receive the same return as a newsletter service.

Newsletters do not incur transaction costs and taxes. They might ignore mutual fund penalties for actively trading, or that a fund may not be available at the brokerage you have accounts with. Not only that, but newsletters often 'forget' their many losing portfolios over time. Their published statistics may leave out those returns.

Financial Products Worth Avoiding

"Protection" Against the Market

Some advisors pitch protection against volatile markets. There are a number of ways that this is achieved, and different strategies that are pitched come in and out of vogue, but they tend to follow the same steps:

Step #1: Find a niche clients wish they would have owned yesterday.

Step #2: Create a fund or product and market it to financial advisors.

Step #3: Advisors sell the idea to clients.

Step #4: When the niche begins to underperform, reassure clients of the reason to own until a new niche is found. Repeat the steps above until the client realizes this is not an intentional investment strategy.

Advisors who work in niches generally see their value to clients as **gatekeepers** to products. They do not invest intentionally, often are commission-based or fee-based (not fee-only) advisors, and will always find new gimmicks to sell that have little to do with your plan.

ETF market timing and option protection

Some money managers go as far as to use certain features of ETFs to market them as *protection* against market declines. The reality is the protection is just another gambling service that in the end does not do what it promises. In over a decade working as an advisor, I have personally witnessed several firms dump these strategies after terrible performance.

Did they give up their gambling and start to give clear and intentional investment advice?

No. They doubled down and created even worse ways to lose their clients' money.

Variable Annuities

Above we mentioned **fixed annuities** can be considered a piece of the Stability category. Fixed annuities may have a place in a portfolio, but one must be very diligent to make sure they are receiving what is in fact a fixed annuity, and be aware of the details and competitiveness of the product.

Variable annuities on the other hand have almost no place in a portfolio. They are sold today with gimmick guarantees of growth (not truth growth) and what they often call *income*.

The following analogy I use with clients about these annuities that basically summarizes how the insurer can *guarantee* high rates of return, and income payouts.

If you have been to any of the major amusement parks of the world, you are likely to be familiar with the character currency that is sold for use in the park, and as trip souvenirs.

The annuity has two accounts – the real value of the money that you put into the annuity (which is then devastated by fees), and the amusement park account that will have guaranteed growth.

The attraction to these products is that the insurer guarantees the amusement park account will 'grow' by an attractive percentage. Your real account value will fluctuate, and be eaten alive by 4-5% and greater fees (recall our chart on the impact of a 1% fee – now multiple that times 4). It is attractive to hear that you will earn 5% 'guaranteed', but one needs to remember this is simply the amusement park account that grows. The importance of this will be seen in a minute.

At retirement, just like amusement park money, the annuity payout buys you significantly less income, to the tune of 30% less or greater.

What does this mean in practical terms? That you could go into retirement with a traditional retirement investment strategy with significantly less money, and you would do better.

At retirement, your Prudential Paper, or Jackson National Bucks don't exactly buy what a normal dollar invested in a normal annuity would purchase. Just like if you bought a Pizza at an amusement park it costs twice as much as a pizza bought on the outside, with real dollars, you not have to purchase your future income with fake dollars that are extremely costly to play with. With the annuity you are agreeing to buy your pizza, gasoline, and everything else from the park, where you must pay an additional 30% simply to access your money. The annuity is less honest than an over-priced amusement park because it takes your money long before it gives you anything in return.

Of course the conversation is never framed like this when the advisor is making a sale. Variable annuities are not bought, they are sold on an unsuspecting client that does not get the full picture from their advisor. You aren't told that your future growth of 6% will only buy you half of the income you could get elsewhere. Or that you could go to Vegas with half of your portfolio and still come out ahead of the variable annuity income stream versus a regular annuity.

No, this information is not shared with the public. In fact, I not only have compared these products, but have ran calculations in the past on a major brokerage firms website that offers both the regular annuity, and the variable annuity. The results I posted as a blog, and although I'm not certain anyone of importance from this particular company reads my lowly blog, but within a month the calculator for the good, old regular annuity was removed from the website. Only the calculator for the variable annuity remained.

It's clear this annuity is a money maker for broker financial-advisors and brokerage companies alike. There are a few other reason it is not the one I would recommend as a fee-only advisor.

Unintentional Investments

You never will have deep conversations with your advisor about the actual investment products that a variable annuity holds, or the strategy it uses to guarantee them. The strategies are a secret; your advisor is not allowed to know them. The investments the annuity company does allow you to choose from can be changed at any point, and they change frequently.

Because of the above, variable annuities could be the least intentional, least clear investment available.

Your Retirement at Risk

Not only do these annuities pay less, hide what they are doing with your money, and take away your ability to control your investments, but they also are unsure themselves if they can pay you back. While I've been writing on the risks of these products for the past five years, companies just within the past few years have cut benefits, raised costs, and publically acknowledged their concerns about the risks these products will place them at in the future.

Variable annuities for a while tried to leapfrog each other on a minimum rate of return they promised investors. But, while they were trying to impress more clients with the large font 5-7% guarantees.

During the market downturn of 2008, many of these firms accepted bailout funds. More increased their fees on current customers in order to deal with risk. Others removed high return and diversifying investments for others that maintained the returns and risk. It is still the case in 2011 that regular new stories run about how companies that offer these variable annuities have overly risky books of business and how many firms have left the market entirely due to the uncertain nature of their future liabilities.

And still advisors sell these higher costing products with no consideration for the risks. This is truly the financial services industry is at its worst.

True protection products and strategies have been available for decades. Never has the conversation about annuities been even a part of the financial advisor vocabulary until variable annuities offered advisors the chance to sell a product that locks up your money for decades, and guarantees your advisor is paid for as long.

Annuities that place your retirement at risk have no place in an intentional portfolio. The income is not intentional, the investment portfolios change and cannot be counted on, and the company itself may be accepting too much risk should the markets falter. These annuities exist for one purpose – to give broker-advisors a product they can offer that consumers cannot purchase on their own. Advisors who offer these typically have a **gatekeeper** mentality – they see their value as being a product provider, not someone whose advice is worth paying for.

It is sad these advisors don't consider the cost to their clients' portfolios, lifestyles, (and their own income) over the life of the products. They are far too concerned about making a quick buck and locking your money away for a very, very long time.

Absolute Return Strategies

If the investment strategy you have uses any of the following words, chances are good you fit into this category:

- Absolute
- Inverse
- Leveraged
- 200, 400, 600, 800; 1.5x, 2x, 2.5x; or other strategies based on numbers
- Hedged
- Enhanced
- Extra

The idea is that a money manager can deliver consistently positive returns above inflation, if only allowed to invest however they want. The manager might put half of the portfolio into Argentinian bonds today, and move it out for Russian oil stocks tomorrow.

I could go on about these products, but I've found the firms that are most adamant about using them fit into one of two groups. The first are extreme Gamblers. This group may have had success in timing the market in managing private money, and believes they can expand their strategy to a retail market.

The problem is that managing private money is not the same as managing retail investments. Retail investing experiences significant inflows and outflows. Successful retail funds grow to such sizes that Gamblers become unable to move in and out of positions without significant cost. In fact, many absolute return funds find that the strategies that made them successful are not possible when your fund is 10-100x as large.

Funds often find success gambling in less liquid markets, where there may not be a significant amount of opportunity to invest a large amount of money. When you are a $10 million dollar fund, and find a way to invest several million dollars for a large profit, it can add nicely to your bottom line. When you are a $1 billion dollar fund, those opportunities may not be worthwhile, and you must test out new gambles in order to achieve similar success.

Or, if you prefer, another way to look at this phenomenon is consider if you were an extremely successful jockey. Now imagine yourself a much larger jockey. You probably are going to have a harder time finding success.

The second group of entrants into the absolute return category are fund managers trying to remake their image. They either have horrible track records at managing relatively simple portfolios, or they were involved in scandals and are attempting to remake their image with a new marketing campaign. The bottom line with this group is they are trying to change some part of their past through a new investing category. They were not stewards of their clients assets, and the risks are that they will continue to place their interests ahead of their clients.

Now they want total control to change on a daily basis not only the stocks, but the amount you have in stocks, the amount in cash, the amount in bonds, and so on.

Fool me once...

I worked with an advisor who recommended people use this in place of their cash reserves. As we've covered by now, there is only one reason an advisor recommends moving your cash into a gamble – extra income for the advisor.

Three pieces of information may further tell the tail, which were all produced around August, 2011. In an Investment News article titled "Alternative-strategy Funds Thrive Despite Spotty Records," Dan Jamieson noted that alternative strategies are mostly sold by advisors rather than purchased by investors[iv]. Financial Planning magazine published an article August 30th, 2011 stating that advisors that use the above strategies purchase several different products; Independent Advisors (hedge funds), bank advisors (limited partnerships), and registered investment advisors (structured products), all recommended products that were unique to their business model. This fit my experience working with a broker who sold mutual fund products. The product fit is often based on an advisor having a unique accessibility to offer that product.

It's clear, these funds are being sold simply as a way for advisors to differentiate themselves, they do not have a clear use in a portfolio.

The above products, as well as other products that typically have to be sold by advisors such as variable annuities, are sold by advisors who require a gimmick in order to sell clients on the value of their services.

Sell When Necessary

Sometimes it can be hard to sell a fund or stock that is down in value. Individuals often have an attachment to funds, and when they are down, they believe it makes more sense to wait for a rebound and *only* **then** will they sell.

We sell or recommend a sale when it is appropriate when looking at the investment mix. If an investment is not appropriate for the mix, if it does not fit the needs of a $G / P / S$ plan, and if for another fundamental reason the investment is no longer desirable, such as the company no longer is seen as a good steward of your money. It is simply not worth the risk of keeping something that is not in line with the rest of your plan.

Holding an investment because it has lost money is not considering it as a part of a portfolio; it doesn't see the forest for the trees. Recall from our Gambling examples, an investment may suffer for a long-time, performing worse than the funds that would have provided a better overall experience.

How Your Manager Feels May Determine Your Returns

The field of behavioral finance is an emerging discipline, but generally I explain it as professionals want to understand why investors don't follow their advice.

But, some have been turning the science on professionals to determine if they are also subject to behavioral trend. Cabot Research, a firm that reviews portfolio managers for behavioral trends, believes there's a lot more we need to know about our investment managers than simply their past performance – such as how they react to market volatility, and if they have conviction in their stock picks.

Cabot often finds that the same bad behaviors that limit the returns of individual investors – not selling winners, not selling losers, overvaluing winners, loss aversion – also impact the returns of professionals.[v]

In an article from the Investment News in July 2011, a financial advisor who sat on the board of a mutual fund stated during the market downturn that even those who are experts at investing at times lost their cool. "They were as fearful and emotional as any investor."

No Fund Company Can Be the Expert at Everything

Our requirements for choosing an investment management firm for our clients is strict. Because of that we limit our recommendations to just a few mutual fund and ETF companies that are exceptional.

Often, an opposing argument will be that no fund company can do everything well.

It's an argument that sounds like it should make sense, but the basis of the argument does not align with principles. It is a Gamblers mentality; that a fund that performs better in the short-run, or that has a higher rating, must be a better investment.

I do not deny that gamblers may at times provide better performance, though as we have shown there are plenty of reasons for this.

What makes a good investment is not performance alone. In our minds a good investment manager is a great steward of our money; they invest it exactly as they would expect to have their funds invested. They treat all of their clients with the same level of care and respect, and realize it is the clients they are there to serve. It is a five star restaurant experience, as opposed to being pushed through a fast food line.

Exceptional stewards make every attempt to lower their own costs of doing business so that their clients retain more of their money. They do not place certain clients above others; recommending one sell an asset and making their retail customers the willing buyer. They realize their growth will come not quick and easy, but from doing the right thing when it may be more profitable in the short-run to drop principles and gamble. In the long-run, there is no cheating the market.

We use the exceptional firms, not the good, the untested, or the lucky. We align ourselves with the very few companies who have proven they hold the same beliefs that they are to be first and foremost stewards of the clients' hard earned money.

We expect a gambler to beat us in a sector for any period of time; generally they have some chance of winning in the short-term, but fail in the long. But the relevant question isn't *if* they achieved a higher return, but *how* they achieved that return. As we have shown, we do not believe it is possible to find that manager ahead of time, and even if you did, you likely are letting them invest unintentionally, to take higher risks to achieve that performance that you as easily could have achieved yourself by intentionally taking on additional risk.

I'll Start Tomorrow

Why start tomorrow? This is what every good intentioned dieter says before they put off their health plan for another day, and then another, and then another.

Start today. Start small. Many advisors will work with clients of all sizes, and can implement easily with core portfolios for clients of just about any size. These portfolios give extremely broad diversification, and at very low costs – costs that only a few years ago would only be available to the very wealthy.

Financial Advisor Strategies to Watch Out For

Dollar Cost Averaging

Many advisors promote placing money into the long-term investment plan slowly rather than all at once.

The truth? It doesn't work, and is simply another form of Gambling.

As a professional that is paid for advice, I should tell you what is in your financial interest rather than what will make you the most comfortable. If during the decision making we decide to accommodate your feelings about investing a sum of money into the market, that is perfectly acceptable. But that should not be a professionals starting point.

If you have money, you are not reducing your risk by dollar cost averaging (DCA) into the market. You are taking a short-term bet that goes against history. Simply buying into the market and holding on generates a better return.

Periodically saving more to your investment plan makes sense, but if you already have the money, then DCA is a loser.

If it makes you more comfortable to buy into the market over time, that is the only reason to engage in a DCA approach. For example, if you inherit a large sum of cash, and would feel better emotionally with slowly putting that money into the long-term plan, that may not be in your financial interest, though it can be in your emotional interest. As an advisor it is my job to separate your emotions from your investments and for that reason I do not recommend a DCA strategy as a starting point.

Further Information:

> *Journal of Financial and Quantitative Analysis* contained an article by George Constantinides entitled "A Note On The Suboptimality Of Dollar Cost Averaging as an Investment Policy."

> ✦ *Financial Services Review* (Vol. 2, Issue 1) by John Knight and Lewis
> Mandell "Nobody Gains From Dollar Cost Averaging: Analytical,
> Numerical and Empirical Results."

Small and International Stocks Should Be Managed Actively (You Should Pay Gamblers in these Sectors of the Market)

Some advisors think that the large company stocks are an efficient market. That there is no way for someone to have exceptional information in the large company space that allow an expert manager.

When it comes to international stocks or small company stocks however, they have a different feeling. And it again sounds like a reasonable story.

The data just does not support it.

We've already addresses a few issues with this theory in general. The first, believers in the small and international Gambler theory state that these markets are simply not efficient. The facts are that markets represent the willingness of many buyers across a globally connected world to buy and sell stocks. Think of the market as millions of price-makers deciding every day what the price of a security will be. These advisors believe that there is no way that millions of individual buyers could possibly price the market correctly.

The next is if stock pickers can't find out enough information on the biggest of the big companies in order to beat the market, what chance is there that they will discover this information on smaller, and foreign companies?

The believers in this theory do have some statistics to make their case. They point to results that were reported on indexes from a decade ago that showed Gamblers beat their respected indices for certain time periods.

Am I wrong then? Do small and international Gamblers actually beat Prudent Buyers?

The problem is that many advisors who believe this have not looked at the issue for several years, and index providers have realized flaws in their data since that time.

We live in a world today where information is often assumed to be correct. It isn't often that we question the validity of data, or whether or not data is applicable.

It wasn't the case 20, 10, even 5 years ago that the data providers kept enough information to weigh these theories. It still isn't the case today in many markets. Many indices leave out failed companies from their results, only showing the winners. This inaccuracy alone means the worst funds of the group were excluded from the index results.

Advisors once noted how that small-cap funds regularly outperformed the Russell 2000 small-cap index.

What was unclear at the time was that the index was beat regularly by other indexes. The subsequent performance of the Russell 2000 index has led to a 2006 Morningstar article to dub it the 'Washington Generals' of indexes, referring to how the index always lost.

Does the fact that Gamblers beat the Russell 2000 mean that Gamblers win? Unfortunately, no. The results changed when funds were placed against an alternative small-cap index such as the S&P Small Cap 600. The S&P Small Cap 600 has regularly beat the Russell 2000, likely due to flaws in the Russell's rebalancing and allowance for companies without a history of profits.

We can see it is critically important to compare Gamblers to the right index. Index providers have entered the market over the past several years in many areas of the market. We now have competing indices for many areas of the world market, and competition has created better indexes. Advisors who still use this as a reason to use Gamblers in the small-cap stocks likely have not looked at the results over the last decade.

Further Information:

➤ Ennis, Richard M., and Sebastian, Michael D. "The Small-Cap Alpha Myth." *The Journal of Portfolio Management*, Spring 2002, pp. 11-16.

➤ Chu, Melinda "Measuring Active Small Cap Manager Performance: Why Benchmarks Matter." Standard & Poor's, July 10, 2002.

Gamblers Win In an Up Market (Or, Just as Often Heard, They Win In a Down Market)

The facts simply are Gamblers don't win. Depending on the bias of your advisor, they may believe that in an upmarket by overweighing winners, or in a down market by avoiding losers or moving to cash, that gamblers can add value. They generally claim to have 'seen it' firsthand.

This is nothing more than a gamblers dream. There have been many studies on this idea. It hasn't proven true.

Vanguard Group found from 1973 until 2011 that active funds beat the Dow Jones U.S. Total Stock Market Index in only two of the last seven bear markets. And in bull markets the results were worse; seven of the eight bull markets since 1971 were won by the index[vi].

Generally what is true is that funds that take more risk do better in up markets, and funds that take less risk do better in down markets.

Now, what I contend should be taken from this is not that the gambler did better or worse, but that the gambler took more or less risk than you hired them to. In other words, what you paid them to provide you was not what they decided to give you.

And how is that intentional?

A more prudent and intentional approach than paying managers to take more or less risk with your money is to take an amount of risk that you mean to. Do it by allocating your money to investments that take just the amount you asked for. Don't pay the high costs of a Gambling manager to get what you didn't want in the first place.

ETFs are a Must Own

The story advisors who sell an ETF approach is that a particular investment product beats another. This isn't quite comparing apples to oranges, since exchange traded funds and traditional mutual funds are BOTH a type of mutual fund. But it is comparing what for the most part is the cream of the crop with a much larger investment pool that includes a lot of losers.

While at Clear Financial Advisors we do use ETFs for parts of our portfolios, proponents who write about the products often overstate their case. Intentionally or not (often in the press I believe it's not) they tend to compare the *average* mutual fund to the *average* ETF.

The real comparison that is made is comparing a Maserati with the average automobile. Clearly the Maserati wins in just about all categories that one could compare. It's not a fair comparison at all to take what so far has been a high-end product (meaning it comes close to fitting many of the low-cost, high quality attributes of a good investment), compare it to the 'average' mutual fund which contains more than its share of high-cost, low quality investments you should avoid.

Journalists I give the benefit of the doubt to, financial advisors on the other hand who tout the advantages of ETFs are often doing it as a marketing gimmick. Many advisors use ETFs for their characteristics that make them easier to Gamble. Since ETFs trade like stocks, they can be Gambled during the day; they are frequently bought to trade in a sector or market for the short-term; and many offer the ability to leverage your gains (and losses).

Bond ETFs

Bond ETFs pose another interesting risk that can materially impact portfolio returns.

Bonds of a particular series do not trade on the market as regularly as stocks. In fact many are not frequently traded at all. Transacting in bonds generally involves placing your bonds out on the open market for a **bid** to the investors who are in the market for bonds at that particular time. Unlike stocks where the prices are relatively known, a bond may not be priced regularly, and so the published value of a bond ETF can vary significantly from the actual value. The iShares iBoxx High-Yield ETF saw its price on the market trade between a 7.9% *discount* to a 12.7% *premium* between October and December of 2008.[vii]

Some would suggest this is the market pricing the holdings in the ETF portfolio. The fact is though that a bond ETF will be managed in a Price-Taking fashion that leaves room for arbitragers to potentially take advantage of unaware investors. A bond mutual fund manager will have a significant advantage in their ability to selectively manage the underlying investments for inflows and outflows.

Summary

ETFs are simply another tool to have in your portfolio. They are a different type of fund; there are characteristics to them that may or may not be beneficial for a given asset class, most of which are neither good or bad. However, they cannot be compared 'on average' to any other investment vehicle, and their Gambling attributes are not the reasons one should own them.

College Savings Plans

Section 529 plans and other 'college' accounts are not all they are cracked up to be. They are an option for college savings, but there are many things to consider before deciding they are the best option. They tend to be presented by mutual fund and insurance companies as the way to save for college, but they fail to meet many ideal investment characteristics.

Reason #1: More so than retirement plans, your investment choices are limited, and they may change at any point without your discretion.

Reason #2: Here is another area that you have a partnership with the government, though this time it includes the federal and state government.

The Upside

The upside is a potential to grow money without paying taxes on gains if that money is used for qualified higher education expenses.

The Downsides

➤ *You are simply paying to not pay taxes for a short time, and use that tax money for college.* Gains and distributions can be managed, and since you give up the potential to use losses on your return, this isn't always a benefit.

➤ *The states and investment providers have made bad gambling bets.* There are plans that basically have guaranteed losses with no true Stability investments. It's common to see plan sponsors be removed from plans (unintentional investing done for you by the states). If you invest through a broker-advisor, most plans they offer today are Gamblers.

➤ *The rules have changed in the past and may continue to change.* State tax deductions have changed, as have rules on transferability, rules on how you can use the money, and so on.

➤ *You have to pay to play.* Just like all of the above changes, can we be sure that the state won't change their costs, or change to a plan where they receive a higher benefit (at your cost)?

➤ *Fees.* Plan fees have come down in recent years, but the fees are still high for no reason. The companies that manage the money already manage billions of dollars in a given strategy at a lower cost. Section 529 plans cost more for no worthwhile reason.

Some argue that the cost is worthwhile. I can't be so sure considering all of the other downsides. Some studies have also shown that investing for college in the aggressive nature of Growth is not appropriate for most of the college savings term, even considering it in the context of $G / P / S$. Just about every 529 plan leans too heavily on Growth despite the risk, and many do so at an inappropriate level even if it is not true.

Other Ways to Save and Pay:

> ➤ *Make it a part of your portfolio.* A low-cost, Prudent Buying approach gives you the flexibility of paying for college in many ways in the future. It allows you to save in the best place to invest today, and use the financing option that is the best for you in the future.
>
> What if the best way to pay for college in the future isn't from your savings? What if the education system changes? What if the college financing system as we know it completely changes?
>
> ➤ *Loans.* You may use loans for college. If loan rates at the time of college are low (say ~2-4%), you may choose to let your portfolio grow for the future, and pay the interest costs (which today may be deductible and therefore are even lower). There are many situations where loans might be dischargeable, depending on the employment sectors your dependent chooses.

Your best place to put the money today may be a tax-advantaged account in your name. You may be able to invest more, have more control, and you may find that the ways to pay for college in the future in the best possible way are not from your personal savings.

Section 529 plans should be viewed as a possible tool for college, but they are not *the only* tool. If you accept that there are risks, costs, and ongoing reporting you will have to retain records for to take the chance at higher returns, and losing control of your investment approach, they are a valid option. It may be clear that I believe there are many options to consider that may provide a more intentional approach, and one that recognizes money saved for college may not be used for college, or the best money to use to pay the tuition bill once it comes.

Sector Investing, Tactical Asset Allocation, and Concentrated Positions

These three ideas are a part of gambling. Advocates believe they can pick parts of the market that will do better than the broad market.

These advisors perform an activity that is just one step removed from individual stock picking. Generally, they write newsletters that tell you how great their performance has been. They often forget about bad performing portfolios in their newsletter or investment management service when reporting results, and regularly rotate you out of an investment portfolio about every five years. The best reason I can tell is that the idea they are selling you on worked the best over the prior five years, and so they create a product today, sell you on an idea (not on actual performance), and by the time out are in, this one has run its course, and there is a new strategy that performs better for the next five years that you can be sure your advisor will be trying to switch you into five years from now.

Look out for the words *hypothetical* performance in any sales material; this means they did not have the strategy, and are simply recommending now because it did well in the past. Before they created their product. About the only time you can even think a hypothetical performance *may* be relevant is if you are investing in a straight index.

The question I can never seem to get an answer to from those that use this strategy is – if these proponents were truly experts at knowing what strategy was best for the future, wouldn't they have created it five years earlier?

That alone should say something about their expertise at predicting how to invest in the future.

Appendices

A.   Growth Gurus

If you are looking for a little stock-picking entertainment, and further proof that stock pickers may not be the gurus we may believe, visit YouTube.com and run a search for videos related to *Jon Stewart and Jim Cramer.*

After the market decline of 2008, Stewart, the host of Comedy Central's *The Daily Show*, took Cramer and his employer CNBC to task for creating an atmosphere of frenzy around stock picking and overemphasizing the market as a way to 'fast money.' To Stewart, it seemed that while the market fell, stock picking 'gurus' like Cramer continued to be optimistic about and hype companies, and specifically several companies that were about to fail such as Bear Stearns and Lehman Brothers.

In a series of comments and interviews, the two exchanged barbs. With increasing assertiveness Cramer backed his position that he called the market decline correctly. After each interview, Stewart responded with more video evidence from Cramer's television program *Mad Money* showing his comments as the market declined. It became clear in a final interview that Cramer was not even defending himself against Stewart's points; he didn't seem aware of what it was Stewart was saying. The stock picks were not defensible. Cramer was only defending his ego.

In a final showdown on Stewart's *Daily Show*, Cramer looked anything but the assertive, confident stock picker. All of the proof of the incorrectness of his past calls is just further evidence that Cramer and other stock pickers at best provide **entertainment**, but they are not who you can count on for your investments advice.

As is probably predictable, the show went on, and gambling in individual stocks certainly has as well. We have been told (by those with an interest in gambling on stocks no less), that it is a 'stock pickers market.' Apparently that means it is a market where stock pickers are continuing to pick and lose their clients' money.

I tell the above story because it was clear to me through the exchange that Cramer had no desire to defend his picks; what he knew was that he needed to defend his ego and reputation, since that is what investors follow him for – his larger than life personality that makes his picks easier to believe. Cramer could have accepted that his crystal ball on the market and economy is no better than anyone else's, that his recommendations are regularly implemented by thousands of investors, and those investors would have lost everything on Bear Stearns and other bets. His concern was less with serving his followers interests, and more making sure his name was defended.

For further information, spend more time searching famous stock pickers on YouTube. Cramer's tactics of denial of the past are no different than any other stock picker. They need to appear confident and correct, no matter what their track record was. I question if they even remember what stock calls they made in the past; it doesn't affect their ability or need to continue to steer investors astray.

But we live in a world where everything is taped, saved, and stored online. Soothsaying stock pickers who once convinced us through their unwavering confidence that they *knew* how a stock would perform today are easily shown to be false prophets.

B. Various Tables of Growth Returns

Distribution of U.S. Market Equity Returns

Distribution of US Market Returns
CRSP 1-10 Index Returns by Year
1926–2010

Positive Years: 63 (74%)
Negative Years: 22 (26%)

In 2008, the US stock market experienced its second worst performance year since 1926.

In 2009, US market performance was in the top quartile of historical calendar year returns.

Annual Return Range	Years (return)
-50% to -40%	1931 (-43.5)
-40% to -30%	2008 (-36.7), 1937 (-34.7)
-30% to -20%	1930 (-28.5), 1974 (-27.0), 2002 (-21.1)
-20% to -10%	1973 (-18.1), 1929 (-14.6), 2000 (-11.4), 2001 (-11.1), 1969 (-10.9), 1962 (-10.2), 1957 (-10.1), 1941 (-10.0)
-10% to 0%	1966 (-8.7), 1932 (-8.7), 1940 (-7.1), 1990 (-6.0), 1946 (-5.9), 1977 (-4.3), 1981 (-3.6), 1994 (-0.1)
0% to 10%	1970 (0.0), 1953 (0.7), 1960 (1.2), 1987 (1.7), 1948 (2.1), 1939 (2.9), 1947 (3.6), 1934 (4.3), 1984 (4.5), 2007 (5.8), 2005 (6.2), 1978 (7.5), 1956 (8.3), 1926 (9.2), 1992 (9.8)
10% to 20%	1993 (11.1), 2004 (12.0), 1959 (12.7), 1952 (13.4), 1968 (14.1), 1965 (14.5), 2006 (15.5), 1942 (16.0), 1964 (16.1), 1971 (16.1), 1986 (16.2), 1972 (16.8), 2010 (17.9), 1988 (18.0)
20% to 30%	1949 (20.2), 1951 (20.7), 1963 (21.0), 1982 (21.0), 1944 (21.3), 1996 (21.4), 1983 (22.0), 1979 (22.6), 1998 (24.3), 1955 (25.2), 1999 (25.3), 1976 (26.8), 1961 (26.9), 1938 (28.1), 1943 (28.4), 1967 (28.7), 2009 (28.8), 1989 (28.9), 1950 (29.6)
30% to 40%	1997 (31.4), 2003 (31.6), 1985 (32.2), 1936 (32.3), 1980 (32.8), 1927 (33.4), 1991 (34.7), 1995 (36.8), 1945 (38.1), 1975 (38.8), 1928 (38.9)
40% to 50%	1935 (44.3), 1958 (45.0), 1954 (50.0)
50% to 60%	1933 (57.1)

CRSP data provided by the Center for Research in Security Prices, University of Chicago. The CRSP 1-10 Index measures the performance of the total US stock market, which it defines as the aggregate capitalization of all securities listed on the NYSE, AMEX, and NASDAQ exchanges. Indices are not available for direct investment; therefore, their performance does not reflect the expenses associated with the management of an actual portfolio. Past performance is not a guarantee of future results.

Distribution of U.S. Market Premium

Distribution of the US Market Premium
1927–2010

Return Premium (Market minus One-Month T-Bills)

Average Annual Premium:
8.04%

Green and orange years indicate 1990s and 2000s respectively.
Data provided by Fama/French. Total US market research factor (total market minus one-month Treasury bills).

Equity Returns of Developed Markets (Non-US)

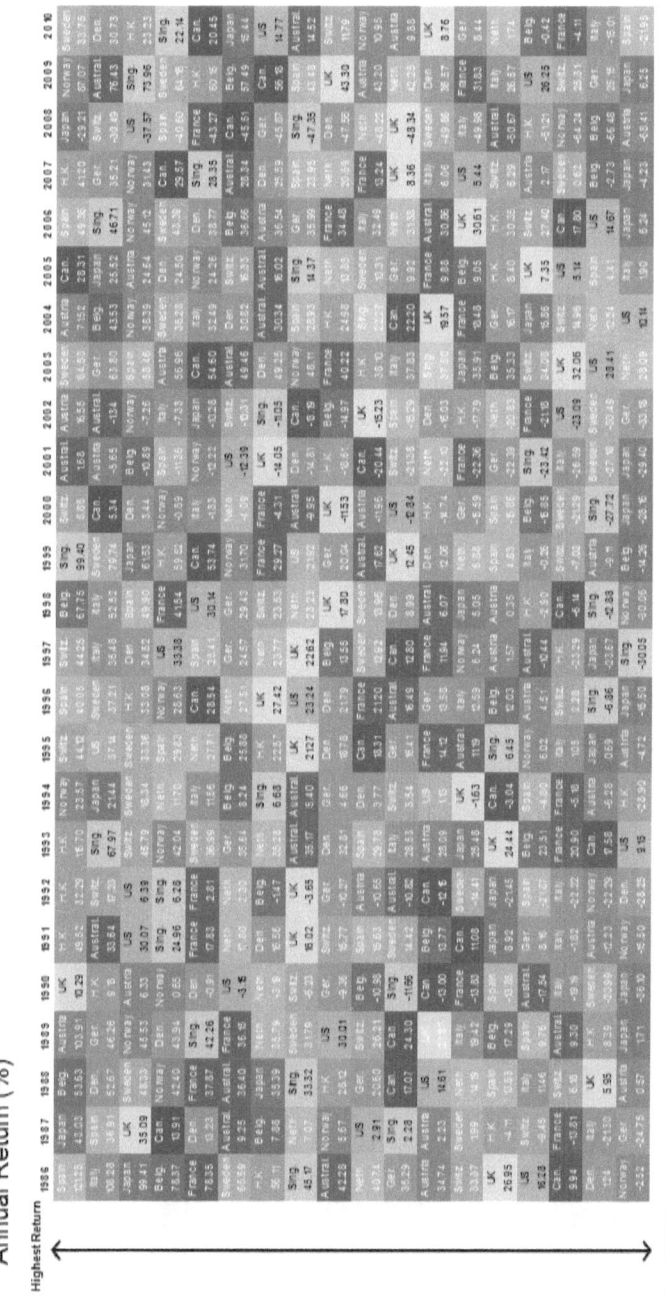

Equity Returns of Developed Markets
Annual Return (%)

In US dollars.
Source: MSCI developed markets country indices (net dividends) with at least twenty-five years of data. MSCI data copyright MSCI 2011, all rights reserved; see MSCI disclosure page for additional information. Indexes are not available for direct investment. Index performance does not reflect expenses associated with the management of an actual portfolio. Past performance is not a guarantee of future results.

Equity Returns of Emerging Markets

Annual Return (%)

	1996	1997	1998	1999	2000	2001	2002	2003	2004	2005	2006	2007	2008	2009	2010
Highest Return	Russia 152.92	Turkey 118.05	Korea 141.15	Turkey 252.41	Czech Rep. 1.82	Russia 55.85	Czech Rep. 44.16	Thailand 144.56	Colombia 132.95	Egypt 161.59	China 82.87	Peru 94.74	Morocco -10.87	Brazil 128.62	Thailand 56.27
	Hungary 107.21	Russia 112.12	Morocco 24.57	Russia 247.06	Poland -4.04	Korea 48.71	Indonesia 42.83	Turkey 125.88	Egypt 126.23	Colombia 107.52	Indonesia 74.63	Brazil 79.99	Colombia -25.10	Indonesia 127.63	Peru 53.35
	Egypt 58.86	Hungary 95.21	Philippines 13.45	Malaysia 114.33	Brazil -11.37	Colombia 45.77	Hungary 30.69	Brazil 115.01	Hungary 92.49	Russia 73.77	Morocco 68.58	Turkey 74.81	Chile -36.37	Russia 104.91	Chile 44.81
	Poland 58.35	Mexico 53.92	Thailand 11.56	Indonesia 93.48	Chile -15.14	Peru 19.92	Peru 30.50	Peru 94.32	Czech Rep. 87.25	Korea 58.00	India 82.55	India 73.11	South Africa -37.89	India 102.81	Colombia 43.41
	Brazil 42.50	Colombia 41.76	Czech Rep. 0.54	Korea 92.42	Malaysia -15.95	Mexico 18.55	South Africa 27.99	Egypt 91.84	Poland 61.52	Brazil 57.05	Philippines 59.65	China 66.24	Peru -40.11	Turkey 98.49	Malaysia 37.01
	Taiwan 40.30	Morocco 35.46	Poland -6.59	Egypt 88.40	South Africa -17.19	Taiwan 10.47	Thailand 27.59	China 87.57	Indonesia 52.21	Turkey 58.94	Russia 55.93	Egypt 58.43	Malaysia -41.21	Chile 98.73	Philippines 35.49
	China 37.46	Egypt 31.23	Hungary -8.16	India 87.35	Mexico -20.49	Thailand 5.25	Colombia 25.36	Chile 84.41	Mexico 48.32	Mexico 49.11	India 51.00	Czech Rep. 55.93	Czech Rep. -42.75	Colombia 84.35	Indonesia 34.62
	Turkey 36.90	Brazil 27.34	Taiwan -20.64	Mexico 80.07	Morocco -21.55	Malaysia 4.56	Russia 15.71	India 78.35	South Africa 44.91	Czech Rep. 46.20	Brazil 45.80	Indonesia 55.03	Mexico -42.94	Taiwan 80.25	South Africa 34.21
	Morocco 36.08	Peru 20.50	India -21.24	Brazil 67.23	India -21.74	Czech Rep. -2.01	Korea 8.82	Indonesia 78.20	Turkey 42.03	India 37.57	Poland 41.93	Morocco 48.15	Taiwan -45.88	Hungary 77.61	Mexico 27.61
	Czech Rep. 30.52	India 11.27	Egypt -27.00	South Africa 57.20	Peru -23.82	Chile -2.83	India 8.38	Russia 75.94	Brazil 36.47	Peru 35.00	Mexico 41.44	Thailand 46.63	Thailand -48.27	Thailand 77.31	Korea 27.15
	Indonesia 27.61	Chile 5.52	South Africa -27.56	Taiwan 52.71	Hungary -26.80	Indonesia -8.49	Egypt 1.59	Colombia 66.93	Chile 29.01	South Africa 28.34	Malaysia 37.14	Malaysia 46.07	China -50.83	Korea 72.08	Taiwan 22.73
	Malaysia 25.55	Taiwan -6.29	Chile -28.50	Thailand 47.16	Russia -30.03	Hungary -9.16	Poland 1.26	Czech Rep. 66.20	Philippines 26.56	Poland 24.36	Czech Rep. 34.59	Philippines 41.88	Philippines -51.87	Peru 72.06	Turkey 21.24
	Mexico 18.70	South Africa -8.18	Malaysia -30.81	Chile 39.01	China -30.54	Morocco -13.70	Malaysia -0.66	Morocco 49.03	Korea 22.86	Philippines 23.92	Hungary 33.70	Korea 32.88	Egypt -52.35	Philippines 67.98	India 20.95
	Philippines 17.75	Poland -22.39	Indonesia -31.53	Poland 31.50	Colombia -38.85	Brazil -16.99	Morocco -8.42	South Africa 45.86	Morocco 22.56	Chile 21.62	Chile 29.33	Poland 25.79	Poland -54.49	China 62.63	Russia 19.40
	Colombia 11.08	Czech Rep. -22.69	Mexico -33.53	Peru 18.86	Egypt -43.71	South Africa -17.21	Mexico -13.81	Philippines 42.76	India 19.11	China 19.77	Taiwan 20.90	Russia 24.79	Korea -55.07	South Africa 57.82	Poland 15.96
	Peru -0.47	China -25.25	Brazil -39.52	China 13.33	Taiwan -44.90	Philippines -19.29	China -14.05	Taiwan 42.55	Malaysia 15.17	Hungary 18.50	South Africa 20.53	Chile 23.68	Brazil -56.06	Mexico 56.63	Morocco 15.33
	India -2.17	Philippines -62.59	Peru -40.22	Hungary 11.86	Philippines -45.01	India -19.45	Chile -19.81	Korea 35.94	Taiwan 9.83	Indonesia 15.76	Egypt 17.08	South Africa 18.14	Indonesia -56.20	Malaysia 52.06	Egypt 12.42
	Chile -13.54	Korea -66.67	Colombia -41.71	Czech Rep. 5.35	Turkey -45.65	China -24.70	Taiwan -24.45	Poland 35.48	Russia 5.69	Morocco 13.97	Colombia 13.76	Hungary 16.80	Hungary -61.53	Poland 42.51	Brazil 6.81
	South Africa -18.06	Malaysia -67.98	China -42.37	Philippines 3.32	Korea -49.52	Poland -27.44	Philippines -28.98	Mexico 32.61	Peru 3.16	Thailand 9.16	Colombia 13.19	Colombia 15.00	Turkey -62.10	Egypt 39.74	China 4.83
	Thailand -36.59	Thailand -73.43	Turkey -52.51	Morocco -11.92	Thailand -56.27	Turkey -32.86	Brazil -30.65	Hungary 32.31	China 1.89	Taiwan 7.25	Thailand 11.61	Mexico 12.15	India -64.63	Czech Rep. 27.77	Czech Rep. -1.86
Lowest Return	Korea -38.14	Indonesia -74.06	Russia -82.99	Colombia -14.38	Indonesia -61.90	Egypt -41.30	Turkey -35.70	Malaysia 26.61	Thailand -0.92	Malaysia 2.29	Turkey -6.97	Taiwan 9.13	Russia -73.83	Morocco -4.98	Hungary -9.58

Source: MSCI emerging markets country indices (gross dividends) with at least fifteen years of data. MSCI data copyright MSCI 2011, all rights reserved. Indices are not available for direct investment. Index performance does not reflect expenses associated with the management of an actual portfolio. Past performance is not a guarantee of future results.

C.   Further Information About Clear Investing

➤ Clear Financial Advisors, LLC – http://www.myclearadvice.com

➤ CFA Market Tools and Research –

http://www.myclearadvice.com/resources

➤ Rob's blog Clear Advice™ - http://www.clearmoneyblog.com

➤ Dimensional Fund Advisors (DFA) – http://www.dfaus.com

➤ Fama and French Forum –

http://www.dimensional.com/famafrench/

ABOUT THE AUTHOR

Robert Schmansky began his career with a financial planning firm specializing in investment management and tax planning for senior corporate management. He subsequently worked as an investment advisor for one of the Midwest's largest independent investment management firms, and a financial advisor at a boutique financial planning firm with senior corporate executive clients before founding Clear Financial Advisors, a fee-only investment and financial planning firm offering accessible services.

Rob is frequently quoted in the media, including the *Wall Street Journal, Forbes, ABC News, Reuters, CNN Money, Chicago Tribune, Dow Jones Newswires, MarketWatch*, National Public Radio, and other publications.

Rob earned a B.S. in human ecology from The Ohio State University, majoring in family resource management, and a M.A. in economics from Walsh College.

Credentials:
CERTIFIED FINANCIAL PLANNER™ (CFP®) professional
Chartered Financial Consultant (ChFC)
Chartered Advisor for Senior Living (CASL)

Participating member of:
Financial Planning Association (FPA)
National Association of Personal Financial Advisors (NAPFA)
Garrett Planning Network -- dedicated to expanding the reach of accessible fee-only financial planning and investment management.

Rob has taught required courses for the CFP® examination as an adjunct instructor at Saginaw Valley State University. He is a contributing writer to NAPFA's Fee-Only Planner's blog at *Forbes* and FPA's blog *All Things Financial Planning*, as well as other publications; and previously was an investment expert for FiLife, a former *Dow Jones/IAC* joint Internet venture.

In his free time, Rob enjoys coaching youth lacrosse, reading fiction, history and biographies, and jogging.

PERSONAL MISSION STATEMENT

"To help clear the financial hurdles that obstruct your best life possible."